How To Do Psychic Readings For Fun & Profit

By Robert Hall

How To Do Psychic Readings For Fun & Profit copyright © 2013 by Robert Hall

All rights reserved. No part of this book may be used or reproduced in any manner whatsoever, including electronically or digitally, without written permission from the author except in the case of brief quotations embodied in critical articles and reviews.

Any Internet references contained in this book were current at the time of publication, but the author cannot guarantee that a specific website or web page will continue to be maintained. Nothing in this book is intended to convey or constitute professional medical, legal, or financial advice.

Printed in the United States of America

Book design by Robert Hall

Cover graphic copyright (c) 2013 Robert Hall

FIRST EDITION

ISBN 978-1482594058

10 9 8 7 6 5 4 3 2 1

Dedication

This book is dedicated to you, dear reader, and everyone else who has heard that small, still voice deep inside, and who has paused to listen, and who has discovered that the small, still voice deep inside is a gateway to a path of great wisdom and real magic.

Thank you for believing in your true self
and trusting your inner guidance.

May your example inspire many others to do the same!

About the Author

Rob Hall is a professional crystal, Tarot and psychic reader, psychic development teacher, and hypnotherapist, specializing in past life explorations, with over 30 years of research, study, experience and teaching development of psychic abilities. He has presented classes and workshops for groups and organizations including the American Board of Hypnotherapy, the Learning Annex, the Learning Light, and the Orange County (California) Chapter of the Mensa Society. He is certified as a professional psychic reader, personal coach, spiritual counselor, and clinical hypnotherapist.

Acknowledgment and Thanks

This book would not have been possible except for the lights of others who helped guide me along the path, including especially Kathy, Katrina, Mary, Miranda, Shelley D. and Shelley N., Susan, and Suzan, as well as such pioneers and luminaries as Dean Radin, Deepak Chopra, and José Silva, who have been such blessings to all of us, and of course all of the rest of my wonderful teachers, students, collaborators, clients, and friends.

TABLE OF CONTENTS

Introduction			1
I.	**Opening Psychic Awareness And Developing Abilities**		3
	1.	Welcome To The World Of The Psychic	4
	2.	Psychic Terms And Phrases	5
	3.	Quiz: Are You Already Using Psychic Abilities?	10
	4.	Your Primary Psychic Sense	13
	5.	Developing Your Other Senses	16
	6.	Determining Your Psychic Symbolism	21
	7.	Variety Is The Spice Of The Psychic Life!	25
	8.	Mastering Meditation	27
	9.	The Magic Of Imagination	30
	10.	Creative Solutions	32
	11.	Using Dream Work For Psychic Development	33
	12.	Some Easy Psychic Practice Workouts	38
	13.	Ethics For Psychic Readers	40
	14.	Cold, Hot, and Warm Psychic Readings	45
	15.	Determining Your Own Code Of Ethics	48
	16.	Creating A Safe Space For Readings	54
	17.	Becoming A Clear Channel	56
	18.	Creating Well-Formed Questions	57
	19.	Ten Potential Causes For Errors In Readings	64

II.	**Psychic Reading Methods, Oracles & Tools**		71
	20.	Methods, Oracles & Tools: An Overview	72
	21.	Cartomancy	74
	22.	Runes	88
	23.	Dowsing With Pendulums, Sticks And Rods	95
	24.	Scrying	101
	25.	Signs And Omens	106
	26.	Automatic Writing	109
	27.	Psychometry	111
	28.	Aura Reading	115
	29.	Direct Psychic Readings	120
	30.	Consulting Higher Self, Spirit Guides And Angels	129
III.	**Doing Psychic Readings Professionally**		133
	31.	Business Basics For Psychics	134
	32.	Setting Fees And Getting Paid	139
	33.	Psychic Business Models And Activities	141
	34.	Locations For Doing Readings	149
	35.	Creating A Powerful Personal Brand	157
	36.	Marketing Your Professional Psychic Practice	164

Conclusion and Further Recommended Reading   182

Introduction

As you may have already discovered, psychic awareness is simply a normal part of the functioning of life. It has been observed and demonstrated in not only humans, but animals as well.

We all have psychic abilities, and we can use these abilities to discover hidden secrets about the past, present and future.

And there are lots of ways to do readings to get psychic information. In this book, we'll explore many of the most popular reading methods so you can find out which methods you prefer, along with helping you to open your everyday psychic awareness.

You may find that psychic readings can be great fun to do with your family and friends!

Some people even "go pro" and make good money as professional psychic readers. Some professional readers earn $100-200 per day, and make a very nice living! At the time of this writing, some top name psychics are charging $800 and more for private readings. Could numbers like these be in your future?

This book is divided into three sections:

In Section I, we will explore how to open your psychic awareness and begin developing your psychic abilities.

Section II discusses ten of the most popular methods for doing psychic readings.

Finally, in Section III, we'll review the basics of becoming a professional psychic reader and load you up with lots of great secrets for success.

So, if you're ready to begin bringing some psychic magic into your life right now, let's get started!

> "We all have some innate psychic ability, but most people never develop it or use it. I am not one of the great psychics you read about in national magazines or see on television. I am just an ordinary person, like you. I taught myself to develop my innate psychic ability ... You will find that this psychic business is really quite simple and friendly and you can progress as far, or as little, as you choose. ... The only requirement is an open mind and a spirit of adventure."
> *~ William W. Hewitt, "Psychic Development for Beginners"*

Section I

Opening Psychic Awareness And Developing Abilities

Chapter 1: Welcome to the World of the Psychic

Welcome to the path of psychic awareness, where you will find deep wisdom and real magic, and the most exciting and enduring adventure of your life!

When a person becomes aware of their true psychic nature, it's one of those things that you simply can't "undo." You can never go back to living a purely material world life and pretending that it didn't happen. Once you've opened the box, and had a glimpse of the sparkling treasures within, your life can never be the same!

Albert Einstein has been quoted as saying, "There are only two ways to live your life. One is as though nothing is a miracle. The other is as though everything is a miracle."

Once we have personally experienced the miracles of our own psychic awareness, we can never again close our eyes to the knowledge of the magical and miraculous beings that we truly are.

So, welcome to the world of miracles! The real miracle is in YOU, and I am thrilled to share this path with you!

Chapter 2: Psychic Terms And Phrases

Let's start by exploring some of the terms and phrases used regarding psychic stuff.

When we use the term "psychic," as in psychic awareness, psychic knowledge, psychic information, psychic readings, etc., what we are talking about is information that we receive other than from *direct observation* or from *inductive or deductive reasoning.*

Direct observation is a situation like: Jim tells you that he is going into the kitchen, you see him go into the kitchen, Jane tells you that Jim is in the kitchen, or you look in the kitchen and – surprise, surprise! - you see that Jim is indeed in the kitchen.

Reasoning or *deduction* involves situations like, you know Jim is in the house, but you can't find him in the bedroom, the bathroom, the living room, the dining room, or the hall, and there's only one other room in the house – the kitchen. So you deduce or reason that Jim must be in the kitchen, even though you haven't seen him in the kitchen or had any other direct evidence that that is where he is.

That is *not* psychic awareness.

An example of psychic awareness would be if you and Jane were at the mall shopping, and you had no contact with Jim at all, but suddenly you knew or had the feeling that Jim was in the kitchen at his house. The "oh wow" moment comes when you call

Jim and say, "Are you in the kitchen?", and he says, "Yes, how did you know that?" These moments will come more and more for you as you journey along the psychic path!

There are two basic ways to receive psychic information - passively and actively.

"Passive" psychic ability comes into play when we receive psychic information unbidden. In this case, the receiver of the information may be focused on an entirely unrelated activity, and then suddenly they receive a certain feeling or awareness.

"Active" psychic ability refers to situations when people actively seek out psychic guidance, such as when a professional psychic performs a reading for a client.

To fully develop ourselves psychically, we need to learn how to open ourselves to passively receiving psychic information as well as developing techniques to obtain information actively.

As humans, we receive psychic information in accordance with the capacities of our beings:

* Mentally, including pictures, sounds, or other awareness in the brain;

* Emotionally, such as when we get unexplained "feelings" about a person or a situation; and

* Physically, which can manifest as a tightness in the stomach area or other bodily sensations, or a sensation of a smell, a taste, or other feeling in the body.

We are actually receiving information on all three of these levels all of the time. While development of psychic awareness is possible on all levels, I have found that most people tend to have a favored method of receiving psychic information.

There are seven common methods - known as the "seven clairs" - by which people receive psychic information:

* Clairvoyance, which involves mentally receiving visual psychic information,

* Clairaudience, which refers to mentally receiving audio information, such as sounds or voices,

* Clairgustance, the sensation of a taste in the mouth,

* Clairalience, or getting the sensation of smelling a scent in the nose (also called clairessence or clairolfacrience),

* Clairsentience, which is a sensation of a physical touch or feeling, like a "gut feeling,"

* Claircognition, which is simply receiving a sudden "knowing" in the mind, and

* Clairempathy, which refers to receiving emotional feelings from other people. People sensitive to this kind of psychic awareness are commonly called "empaths".

When we receive psychic information, it may be about:

* Current events,

* Future events (psychic knowledge of future events is called "precognition," or a "premonition"), or

* Past events (psychic knowledge of past events is called "retrocognition").

Some people may also have psychic communications with other living people or entities. This kind of communicating is referred to as "telepathy."

"Mediums" are psychics who communicate with spirits of those who have died.

While psychic abilities may appear to be more accessible to some people than others, we all have these abilities to some degree, and we certainly have the power to increase these abilities.

> "Most of us are in touch with our intuition whether we know it or not, but we're usually in the habit of doubting or contradicting it so automatically that we don't even know it has spoken. The first step is to pay more attention to what you feel inside, to the inner dialogue that goes on within you."
> ~ *Shakti Gawain*

There are some exercises in the following sections that will help you open your psychic faculties. A key point that you must know is that developing psychic awareness is not so much about increasing a capability as it is about reducing the way that the conscious mind distorts and generalizes the incoming information, and opening channels of communication between different parts of the mind.

It is not really about "effort," or "trying," or "working." It is about *letting go*. It is about *allowing*. It is about getting your brain to stop chattering for just a moment so that you can hear the whispered wisdom of your psychic soul.

Remember, we are already receiving lots of psychic information all of the time. The only reason that we may not be aware of this information is because of the constant chattering of our brains.

When we learn how to quiet our minds then psychic awareness will come to us easily and naturally.

> "The possibility of stepping into a higher plane is quite real for everyone. It requires no force or effort or sacrifice. It involves little more than changing our ideas about what is normal."
> ~ *Deepak Chopra*

Chapter 3: Are You Already Using Psychic Abilities?

I have discovered that many people have already had psychic experiences, but they just didn't recognize the psychic nature of those experiences.

Consider the following questions. Have these things happened to you before? If so, it may be that your psychic awareness has already begun to open!

* Have you ever had a premonition of an event which later proved true?

* Have you ever had a dream that came true (whether in part or whole)?

* Have you ever met someone or had someone come to visit you and you had recently had thoughts about that person or otherwise anticipated the meeting or visit?

* Have you ever successfully followed your "gut instinct" in a game or business deal?

* Have you ever thought about a person or felt you were going to hear from a person and then received a telephone call or other communication from that person?

* When an item has been lost, have you ever had a successful feeling as to where it was located?

* Have you and another person ever both said the same thing at the same time?

* Have you ever noticed a recurring "theme" during a time in your life, such as things having similar numbers or names?

* Have you ever had feelings of sadness that you later discovered coincided with a negative event that happened somewhere else?

* Have you ever experienced "deja vu", where you were in a new place or situation but felt that in some way you had been in that place or situation before?

* Have you ever subconsciously been aware that someone was staring at you and caught them at it?

* Have you ever had particularly strong or vivid dreams?

* Have you ever had a song in your head and soon after heard it on the radio or in a store?

* Has the solution to a problem ever come to you in a flash of insight?

* Do you sometimes know the time without looking at a clock? Or do you sometimes wake up just before your alarm goes off?

* Has someone ever told you some information and you realized that you already knew it?

* Have you ever experienced "synchronicity", where things seem to happen just when you need them to happen?

With regard that last question, I want to say that synchronicity is one of my favorite things about leading a psychically aware life. It always seems so magical when the exact thing I need just drops into my life right when I need it, *and it happens all the time!*

And very soon it may be happening for you, too!

Chapter 4: Your Primary Psychic Sense

We all have a preferred physical sense, and we all have a preferred psychic sense. Each of us has a "special gift" - a way that we most easily obtain psychic information. It may be by visions, hearing a guiding voice, getting a "gut feeling," and so forth.

Discovering your own strongest psychic sense will not only help you become more aware of the information that you receive by that method, but it will also alert you to other areas that may need more attention and development.

Consider the following for a moment:

* Which sense do you rely on most when you're having a new experience? Sight? Sound? Feeling?

* If you had to lose one of your senses, which one would you most prefer *not* to lose?

* When you consider your memories, what sense predominates? Images? Sounds? Feelings? Smells?

* Do you reveal your preferred sense in your language? When you're talking to visual people, you may hear them use phrases like: "That looks good," "I can see what you mean," or "I want to get the big picture."

Auditory, hearing-oriented people may say things like: "That sounds right," "It's clear as a bell," or "I hear what you're saying."

Kinesthetic, feeling-oriented people often make comments like: "This feels right to me," "I'm getting a handle on it," or "I'm really warming up to this idea."

No matter which sense you prefer, there are many millions of people who share that same method. So, there is no right or wrong answer. There is only your answer, for yourself.

Still not sure? Here's a simple exercise in imagination that might help.

Put your body into a comfortable, relaxed position.

Take a deep breath, and as you let it out count down in your head: Three . . . Two . . . One . . .

And just relax.

OK, now imagine that you are enjoying a day at the beach.

It is a beautiful, warm day . . .

Slowly walk down the beach towards the ocean . . .

Notice how you feel about being at the beach . . .

Watch the waves as they roll and pound on the shore . . .

Hear the squawking of the seagulls flying overhead . . .

Feel the strong ocean breeze on your face . . .

Smell the salt in the air . . .

Hear the laughter of children playing nearby . . .

Feel the warm sand beneath your feet . . .

See the sunlight glistening on the waves . . .

Check your feelings and notice how this moment feels . . .

There is a food vendor selling hot dogs, hamburgers, cotton candy and other foods nearby.

Smell the delicious odor of the food in the air . . .

Go to the stand and get your favorite, just the way you like it. Imagine taking a big bite of the food . . .

Taste the food in your mouth . . . Yummy!

While you were imagining this, did you notice if it was easier for you to imagine some parts than others?

Was it easier to imagine the visual parts, like watching the waves or seeing the sunlight glistening? Or the auditory parts, like the squawking of the seagulls or the children laughing? Or the feeling parts, like the sand beneath your feet or the ocean breeze on your face?

Whichever was easiest - visual images, sounds, or feels - that's your preferred sense. And you will likely find that you will receive your strongest psychic impressions in the same way.

Chapter 5: Developing Your Other Psychic Senses

Some people, upon discovering their preferred sense, wish that it was different. Visual people may want to hear a guiding voice in their mind. Auditory people may wish that they were able to feel a "gut instinct." And kinesthetic, feeling people may wish that they could get visions in their minds.

Once you have discovered your preferred or primary sense, though, then you can begin consciously exploring and developing your skills in the others.

If you are a "visual" person, you can try paying closer attention to sounds, and the tone and other qualities of speech that people use when talking to you, or feelings, and the sensations that you feel with your body.

If you are primarily an "auditory" sound-oriented person, experiment with experiencing the world more through your eyes, your feelings, or your faculties of smelling and tasting.

If your natural preference is for kinesthetic feelings (such as getting a "gut feeling"), there are ways that you can work on developing your other abilities, too.

Try this: hold a small object in your hand and look at it closely. Then close your eyes and try to "see" that same image in your mind. Or listen to a sound clip several times, and then try to imagine hearing that same sound.

It may be a little challenging to start, but the more you practice the easier it will become.

Here's more you can do to wake up your psychic senses. For the next 30 days, and then at least once a week after that, take a few minutes to actively engage each of your sensory organs.

Really take the time to do these exercises properly and you will expand immensely your power to receive psychic guidance.

*   **Touch:** Touch different substances and materials with your fingertips, your face, your hands, your feet, or any other part of your skin and notice the feelings that you get.

How does concrete feel? How does sand feel? How does grass feel? How does dirt feel? How does cloth feel? How does water feel?

Take just a few minutes each day to explore different textures and really examine the feelings that you get through your faculty of touch.

*   **Smell:** "Sniff around" and explore your olfactory senses. Almost everything has a smell - but many of them are quite subtle. Avoid places with strong smells like kitchens or perfumeries.

What is the smell of the tree? What is the smell of the water? What is the smell of grass, a peach, a new shirt, or dirt? Can you smell a difference in the air just before or after a rain storm?

Have fun and expand your experiences with this sense. Most of us do not pay much attention to the sense of smell, but smells that trigger memories and associations can have a powerful impact on us without much conscious awareness on our part.

*   **Taste:** Go beyond your normal experiences and try all kinds of new things. Especially, explore new herbs and spices and vegetables and fruits. Savor the flavors on your tongue, and get to know them well.

You undoubtedly have your favorite meals, but try different ones just for the pure adventure of getting to know different tastes and flavors. Have fun with it!

*   **Hearing:** You can explore this sense almost anytime, anywhere. *Take note of the subtle sounds beneath the obvious ones.* Your subconscious is hearing everything that enters your ears at all times, from the sound of your heartbeat to the squeak of your shoes as your move them.

Notice your ability to use the power of selection in listening and reduce other sounds to focus on just one. For example, the way that you can focus on a particular conversation at a noisy party.

So we can be selective in what we hear, but we can also open to psychic awareness and really start listening to the world around us. Enjoy exploring this extraordinary power you have!

*   **Sight:** As most people are visually-oriented, this may be the most challenging, but *try to look at what you normally don't look at.*

If you usually look up, try looking down. If you normally look at the faces or clothing of people in the street, try looking at how they hold their arms, or move their shoulders or legs.

Notice the shadows of objects or people instead of looking directly at them. Or observe them in a reflective surface, such as a plate glass window. Or just let your eyes defocus a bit and become aware of simple shapes and colors, rather than details.

An Exercise In Imaginative Sensing

Clearly imagine in your mind a freshly cut block of wood.
Project your imagination inside the block of wood.
Take special notice and observe:
*   What does it look like inside the block of wood?
*   Do you hear any sounds?
*   What does it feel like?
*   Does it have a noticeable smell or taste?

Now clearly imagine a solid rubber ball.
Project your imagination inside the rubber ball.
Take special notice and observe:
*   What does it look like inside the rubber ball?

* Do you hear any sounds?
* What does it feel like?
* Does it have a noticeable smell or taste?

Now clearly imagine a large, beautiful, glistening crystal. Project your imagination inside the crystal.
Take special notice and observe:
* What does it look like inside the crystal?
* Do you hear any sounds?
* What does it feel like?
* Does it have a noticeable smell or taste?

While these exercises may seem kind of silly or weird, they are actually very important to do for psychic development.

Do them at least once a week or so, and feel free to play around and come up with your own variations.

They will help you to experience the world in different ways, and you will also be developing your psychic senses along with your physical ones.

Chapter 6: Determining Your Psychic Symbolism

Psychic information is often symbolic. This may be because the information generally comes from the right side of the brain, which is usually the non-language-dominant side, and which therefore tends to communicate in images, sounds, and feelings.

The purpose of this section is to anticipate your personal symbolism. By determining ahead of time what various symbols may represent to you psychically, you may recognize them more easily when you later receive them in a reading.

For example: I may ask for a vision in response to a question, and I may see a knight in a suit of armor.

While this image may seem like a positive one to some people, it may be that a vision of a knight in armor represents (to me) a "challenge" or "obstacle," which would obviously not be a positive response to the question.

If I've figured this out in advance, then when I get a vision of a knight in armor then I know, "oops, there's an obstacle." If I haven't figured this out in advance, then we have to decipher the symbolism of the vision whenever I get it.

Again, much of the psychic information you will get may be symbolic, and there will be times when you just have to note the information that you got and try to figure out what it means.

But it can save much time and effort if you can figure out in advance the kinds of symbols that your psychic mind may commonly use to reflect a particular meaning or message.

For this exercise, on the next couple of pages I've given you a list of words that may commonly arise in psychic work. You may think of some other ones and add them to the list.

For each word, just focus on the word for a moment, and then write down all the impressions that you associate with the word.

These may be images, physical sensations, sounds, smells, tastes, emotional feelings, or even other words .

In the future, if these images, sensations or feelings arise when you are accessing psychic guidance, you should consider whether they are meant symbolically to represent that word.

For example, when I think of the word "yes," some of the associations that I get with that word are: a smile, a feeling of lightness (not heaviness), and a sunny sky.

So if I am doing a psychic reading for someone, and their question can be answered by a "yes" or "no" response, and I get a vision of a smile and a feeling of lightness, then it very well could be that the answer to their question is "yes."

Finally, keep in mind that there are no right or wrong answers - just your answers. If your symbol for "yes" is a vision of a brown dog, or a tingling feeling in your left hand, or the smell of bacon, then *that's* your symbol for "yes," and *that's* the symbol you should notice when you are receiving psychic guidance.

Word List	Associations
Yes	_____
No	_____
True	_____
False	_____
Winning	_____
Losing	_____
Rich	_____
Poor	_____
Happiness	_____
Sadness	_____
Gain	_____
Loss	_____
Growing	_____
Reducing	_____
Good Health	_____
Injury/Disease	_____
Light	_____
Dark	_____
High	_____
Low	_____

Beginning _____

Ending _____

Clear _____

Muddled _____

Good _____

Bad _____

Friend _____

Enemy _____

Love _____

Marriage _____

Success _____

Failure _____

Satisfied _____

Needy _____

Open _____

Closed _____

Obstacles _____

Future _____

Past _____

Life _____

Death _____

Go _____

Stop _____

Chapter 7: Variety Is The Spice Of The Psychic Life!

The Right-Brain Left-Brain theory was developed in the early 1980's as a result of observations of patients after brain surgery.

In general, the theory says that the left part of the brain usually handles tasks involving logic, language and analytical thinking, and the right side of the brain is better suited to tasks involving creativity and personal expression.

Intuition and psychic awareness are commonly considered to be right-brain functions. So, we can strengthen our psychic awareness by making an intentional effort to regularly access and use the right side of the brain.

In the next few sections, we'll explore three powerful tools for living more of a right-brain dominant life: meditation, using imagination, and increasing our creativity.

One simple thing that we can do right now to get our right-brains more active is to break old mental habits and start doing things differently in our lives.

When we use the same mental patterns over and over and allow our minds to fall into repeated rituals, we strengthen those neural pathways but we lose alternative connections between cells in our brains.

However, when we actively choose to engage in new behaviors we force the brain to form new connections. And the more connections we have between our brain cells, the more information we can receive.

We can take advantage of this by simply changing any of the hundreds of rituals in our lives.

If you normally read the newspaper at breakfast, try listening to the radio at breakfast and taking the newspaper to work with you instead. If you usually take a certain route to work, try taking a different route. If you always watch television at a certain hour, try skipping it and reading a book instead. If you always listen to certain kinds of music, then start adding other kinds to your music library. If you always go to certain restaurants or eat certain kinds of food, do something different. *Whatever your habits and rituals may be, try doing something different.*

Anything that you do that deviates from your normal routines forces your brain to deal with the new situation and get creative and learn new things, and to develop new connections between the cells.

Breaking old habits and doing things differently will not only help with your psychic development, but it will actually improve your brain overall! And that's a really good thing!

So do something different!

Chapter 8: Mastering Meditation

Meditation is a practice of relaxing and quieting the mind to help us open ourselves to receiving psychic guidance.

In a survey of several thousand psychics and mediums, over 90% of them said that regular meditation was "necessary" for psychic development.

Learning how to meditate so that we can turn off our inner voice, if only for a few moments, is one of the most important key skills that we can develop on our path to full psychic awareness.

Why? Because what that voice is doing, through its constant chatter, is *creating your reality.* It is telling you over and over again about the material world and reinforcing your beliefs about, and thus your experience of, that world.

So, when we can get that voice to stop, all of a sudden your sense of reality opens up, and literally anything can happen. Deepak Chopra refers to this as moving into "the gap," a place between thoughts, a place of "pure potentiality."

When our inner chatter goes silent then we can hear the still small voice of true psychic awareness or deep spirituality. It's a wonderful, wonderful thing, and well worth mastering.

Following are some popular methods of meditations. All of these should be done in a comfortable, relaxed position, either sitting or lying down, with eyes closed.

*   **Relaxation Meditation:** Starting at your feet and working your way up to your head, focus on and relax each individual set of muscles throughout your body - feet, calves, thighs, lower abdomen, chest, shoulders, arms, back, neck, jaw, face, eyes, and scalp. Give attention for a moment or two to each area to make sure that it becomes totally relaxed.

*   **Breath Meditation:** Simply focus on your breathing. Draw air in through your nose, pull it all the way down to your lower abdomen, hold it for a few seconds, and then let it out through your mouth. Repeat throughout the meditation.

*   **Mantra Meditation:** Select a "mantra" - any word or phrase upon which you wish to focus - and repeat it over and over aloud or silently in your mind during the meditation.

*   **Musical or Guided Meditation:** Play a CD featuring a musical or guided meditation and just let go and follow the music or instructions with your mind.

*   **Proactive Meditation:** Go into a relaxed state of mind and then proactively imagine a desired process. Such processes might include intentionally raising your bodily vibrations, effecting healing processes, astral travel, obtaining psychic information, etc.

I find the breath and mantra meditations to be the best for "turning off the voice" in my head. This is because I'm giving that voice something to do, such as counting breaths (I usually do 4 counts in and 4 counts out) or repeating a mantra over and over.

If you do the mantra meditation, the mantra can be anything you want - it doesn't have to be a lengthy sanskrit saying. You can just repeat the word "peace," or "love," or a short phrase like "I am psychic" or "I open to spirit," or whatever feels best to you.

Chapter 9: The Magic Of Imagination

"Imagination is more important than knowledge. For knowledge is limited to all we now know and understand, while imagination embraces the entire world, and all there ever will be to know and understand."
~ *Albert Einstein*

Another important part of psychic development is engaging the right brain by accustoming our minds to receiving information in unusual ways - that is, by using our imaginations.

By exploring and playing with alternative perspectives through the use of imagination, we actively open and broaden our minds to other ways of learning, understanding, and knowing.

Children often engage in roleplaying, playing with dolls, or talking with imaginary friends. While these types of activities may seem silly to us as adults, they are actually powerful ways to keep our imaginations alive, and our psychic abilities active.

Here are some exercises we can do to give our imaginations a little workout, but there are many, many more.

* Start out easy: read some fairy tales or watch some fun childrens' movies. Let yourself really get involved in the story.

* If you had an imaginary friend, what would that friend be like? (Remember, in the movie *Harvey*, Elwood P. Dowd's imaginary friend was a six foot, three and a half inches tall rabbit!)

* If your family, friends, or co-workers were animals, what kinds of animals would they be? Would one of them be a monkey, or perhaps a peacock, or maybe a lion, or a bear?

* Make up a story about the next stranger you see. Where do they work? Where are they going? What will they do?

* Always be open to new experiences of "reality." What is the taste of victory? What is the sound of blue? What is the feel of truth? What is the smell of happy?

* If you could, what superpowers would you give to five people that you know? The power to fly? Super-strength? The power to be invisible, or to travel through time?

* Anthropomorphize (attribute human personality to something not human) lots of stuff. Have you ever said, or heard someone say, "this drawer doesn't want to go in" or "I think this chair actually wants to be over there instead of over here" or "this stupid thing doesn't want to work"? That's anthropomorphizing!

Ancient peoples used to attribute personalities to the sky, the earth, rivers, the ocean, stones and crystals, and much more. Not only is anthropomorphizing historic, but you may find that it can actually yield some interesting psychic results!

What mood is the sky in today? What clothes want you to wear them today? What secrets can the trees tell you? What does your car want to do? When you're driving, what does the car in front of you want to do?

Chapter 10: Creative Solutions

We've been talking about ways to increase our use of the right side of the brain as well as improve the connections between the two brain hemispheres. Exercising your creativity is another fun method to give your right brain a great work-out.

There's lots of ways to be creative. Here's just a few ideas, but I'm sure you can think of more:

* Drawing, painting or making collages
* Sculpting
* Making crafts or jewelry
* Sewing or needlepoint
* Cooking (put aside the cookbook and have fun!)
* Dancing
* Writing fiction
* Playing musical instruments
* Improvisational acting

Any other kind of activity in which we use our hands or bodies to create something is great for this.

Try to find free-form ways of expressing your creativity, where you can really let your feelings go where they want and get your creative juices flowing.

And make some beautiful art or some great music while you're at it! Let your inner artist come out and get a little bit wild!

Chapter 11: Using Dream Work For Psychic Development

"Dream work" generally refers to programming your dreams, and having lucid dreams. In dream work, we can accomplish awesome and amazing things in our lives.

In order to "program" our dreams, we give our minds instructions as to what kind of dreams we want to have, and then we make sure that we receive the message that we requested.

A "lucid dream" is a dream where you are aware that you are dreaming. The cool thing about this (when it happens) is that it gives you the power to inject intent into the dream and, to a certain extent, control the dream. You can go places that you've wanted to visit, meet people (almost anyone) that you've wanted to meet, learn amazing secrets, and so much more.

(Note: Is your goal to interpret a dream? Don't waste time or money on books that claim to offer interpretations of dreams. All dreams are intensely personal, and these generic one-size-fits-all dream interpretation books will be of no help. Instead, program a dream asking for clarification of your previous dream.)

To program a dream, make sure to keep a pen and paper by your bedside, and when you turn off the light and get ready to sleep, repeat three times to yourself the instructions for the dream that you want (and it really can be anything that you want). For example:

"Tonight I will dream about ways I can improve my psychic abilities, and I will remember my dreams."

"Tonight I will dream about how I should promote my business, and I will remember my dreams."

"Tonight I will dream about meeting my spirit guides, and I will remember my dreams."

"Tonight I will dream about the person I will marry, and I will remember my dreams."

"Tonight I will dream about the perfect way for me to make a lot of money, and I will remember my dreams."

Clearly, there is really no limit as to how you can program your dreams!

Then, *first thing when you wake up*, before you use the restroom or get your coffee or whatever, write down everything that you remember about your dreams. You can always take your time later to try to interpret or understand the dreams, but you must write down what you received immediately.

Don't understand the meaning of the dreams you got? Again, program another dream asking for clarification of your previous dream. Keep doing this until the meaning of your original dream is clear.

To have lucid dreams, it is also very simple, although it may take a few tries for success.

Repeat to yourself several times during the day: "Lucid dreaming is easy for me."

Also, several times during the day, open your hand and look at the palm of your hand.

When you turn off the light to go to sleep, repeat three times to yourself: "I will know when I am dreaming." Then go to sleep.

When you next have awareness, open your hand and look at the palm of your hand. Notice whether you are really looking at the palm of your hand or doing it in a dream.

If you're doing it in a dream, great - you are lucid dreaming! Go ahead and do whatever it is that you wanted to do in a lucid dream.

But if you're just looking at your real palm, then you are still awake - go back to sleep!

> "Why are people interested in learning to be conscious in their dreams? According to my own experience, and the testimony of thousands of other lucid dreamers, lucid dreams can be extraordinarily vivid, intense, pleasurable, and exhilarating. People frequently consider their lucid dreams as among the most wonderful experiences of their lives.
>
> "If this were all there were to it, lucid dreams would be delightful, but ultimately trivial entertainment. However, as many have already discovered, you can use lucid dreaming to improve the quality of your waking life. Thousands of people have written to me at Stanford telling how they are using the

knowledge and experience they have acquired in lucid dreams to help them get more out of living."
~ *Stephen Laberge, psychophysiologist and author*

You can also use dreams to learn about a divination tool, like a Tarot deck or a crystal.

Here are the steps:

If your subject is something sturdy, like a crystal, you can put it under your pillow. If it's something kind of fragile, like a Tarot card, I suggest you put it at your bedside instead.

Put a pen/pencil and some paper at your bedside as well.

When you're ready for bed, take the subject item in your hands and say to it (either out loud or mentally), three times, "Send me a dream that will best teach me how to learn from you" or "best strengthen our relationship" or "teach me your secrets" or whatever you feel is most appropriate.

Then put the item either under your pillow or at your bedside, or wherever you decided to put it.

Finally, right before you fall asleep, say to yourself (either out loud or mentally), three times, "Tonight I will remember my dreams." Then, right when you wake up, immediately write down everything you remember from your dreams.

During the following day, reflect on whatever you received in your dreams, and try to understand how your dreams may have answered your request.

Usually, whenever I use this technique, I get amazing stuff in my dreams. (I always do it when I get a new crystal or Tarot deck.) I may not always immediately understand what the dream means or how it applies, but the dreams are often very vivid and interesting and give me lots of interesting insights.

If, after a few days, the meaning of your dreams has still not become clear to you, you can try repeating the exercise and asking for a dream that clarifies your first dreams.

Chapter 12: Some Easy Psychic Practice Workouts

Besides doing readings, there are some other easy ways you can exercise your psychic abilities.

* Shuffle a deck of cards and go through about 10 cards and guess whether they are black or red. Put the ones you guess to be black into one pile, and the ones you guess to be red in another. When you're done, turn them over and see how you did.

* When you get good at the first exercise, then try guessing whether a card is a face card (jack, queen or king) or a "pip" card (ace to ten).

* Get some dice and roll one die and guess if it will be odd or even.

* Horse races: Go to a website for a popular racetrack and download or printout a list of the horses that will be racing on later dates. Psychically guess (or use a tool like a pendulum to find out) which horse will win each race. Then check back later and find out which horses actually won each race. Get good at this one and you can make a nice little income on the side!

* If you go to school or a job, guess what colored clothing your fellow students or co-workers will be wearing tomorrow.

* If you're in a position where you meet different people every day, try guessing who you will meet tomorrow.

* When your phone rings, guess who is calling you.
* When facing a choice of two or more paths or directions in life, imagine taking each path in your mind. Really try to imagine each one fully and vividly. Notice which path seems easier or harder to imagine, clearer or murkier, or which path feels more comfortable or "right" than the other in your mind. (This is actually a very powerful way to get psychic information. Try and practice this one a lot, so that you get good at it.)

These "mini" psychic workouts will keep your abilities in good shape and tone, and they're fun to do!

Chapter 13: Ethics for Psychic Readers

In our work as psychic readers, we can wander into a lot of areas that may invoke consideration of ethical issues.

While some people may consider psychics to simply be "scammers," and thus entirely unethical, for those of us who try to walk this path with integrity and honor, we do need to consider all potential ethical issues when providing our services.

Issues that ethical psychics might consider include:

* Whether to make any predictions regarding the four Ds (death, divorce, disease and disaster)
* Client confidentiality
* Confidentiality of 3rd parties
* Setting your boundaries
* Detaching from clients for clear readings
* Issues regarding cold, hot, or warm readings
* Dealing with addicted clients
* And much more

When someone comes to us for a reading, whether it's a paying client or just a friend, a relationship is formed. They are trusting us to provide them with information regarding special or private aspects of their lives. In response to the trust that they give us, we need to respond by treating them ethically.

In my own experience, the vast majority of practicing psychics are good, honorable, and ethical people. At some point in their lives they discovered that they had a special gift, and they simply want to share that gift with others.

Sadly, there are a few people in this world who observe the trust that people give to psychics, and they scheme to create a way to take advantage of those people.

One of the most famous schemes involves an "upsell," which is an expense beyond the cost of the reading. The psychic tells the client that there is a curse on the client, or that the client is possessed by an evil spirit, or that something bad is going to happen to the client. However, <u>for an additional fee</u>, the psychic can remove the curse, get rid of the evil spirit, and so forth.

Some people judge all psychics by the actions of the few bad ones, and that is unfortunate. After all, there are bad doctors, lawyers, priests, judges, politicians, and so forth, as well. An entire community should not be condemned because there are a few bad apples in the barrel.

Also, not all ethical issues are the result of bad intentions.

For example, many psychics do not tell a client if they get a premonition of what we call the "four Ds" - death, divorce, disease and disaster. This is because, for example, by telling the client that it looks like they will be getting divorced in the next year, such a prediction can become a self-fulfilling prophecy, as the client may go home and look for evidence that their mate is unfaithful and thus begin the destruction of the relationship.

Instead, these psychics may advise their clients that they foresee a "difficulty" or a "challenge" and help the client find ways to overcome or get around the difficulties or challenges.

And such things may indeed be overcome. Things we learn psychically are *not* always set in stone as far as the future goes; they often only portend what will happen *if* everything continues to go in the same direction that they are going now.

For example, in the book "The Palmistry Workbook" (The Aquarian Press, 1984) by Nathaniel Altman, there is a photograph of the palm of a man's hand that indicated a break in the lifeline at about age 65. The man took the warning seriously, and changed his health and lifestyle habits. A later photograph shows the break in the lifeline had mended itself.

An unintentional source of ethical issues may arise when a client becomes addicted to getting readings or to us personally. While we may be flattered by the attention, or while we may enjoy the steady flow of money, at some point we should stop and consider whether it is ethical for us to allow that to continue or whether we are becoming a part of the problem.

Psychics may also encounter ethical issues if they become emotionally involved with a client, by feeling empathetic, perhaps, or pity. While we are all human, and can be moved by a sad story, these feelings can interfere with our ability to do a good reading. We'll talk more about this issue in Chapter 17 about "Becoming a Clear Channel."

Another ethical issue that can come up is whether or not to use our psychic abilities to "spy" on third persons without their knowledge or consent.

You may sometimes find that clients come to you and ask questions like: "Does *X* really love me?" "Is *X* cheating on me?" or "Is *X* going to leave his wife for me?"

For me, psychic spying on third persons without their knowledge or consent breaks my ethics, and I won't do it; however, I am sensitive to the client's situation as well.

For example, perhaps someone comes to me who is involved with a married man. He has been telling her that he loves her, and that he will (sometime) leave his wife for her, but not just yet. The client is afraid she is being played for a fool.

I won't try to spy on the man's feelings or intentions, because it is against my ethics.

However, I <u>can</u> look into the client's future to see if she and the man will marry, or if she will end up in a different relationship, or if she will have her heart broken in this relationship. These are all questions that are about *her*, and she is giving me her consent to explore these issues psychically, so there is no ethical problem.

I just want you to be aware of the possibility that ethical issues may arise in your work as a psychic. I believe that the best thing is to consider these kinds of situations *before* they come up, and how you want to handle each one ethically, so that when they do come up you already know what to do and you can keep your ethics strong.

Chapter 14: Cold, Hot, and Warm Psychic Readings

"Cold," "warm," and "hot" psychic readings are various types of fake or false psychic readings, and generally *not* ethical. The only ethical use that I can think of would be a "mentalist" magic act, in which the performer used the techniques to fake an actual psychic reading for purposes of entertainment, and clearly informed the audience about the nature of the act.

"Cold" Readings

"Cold" readings are readings in which the "psychic" simply recites generic statements that could apply to almost anybody. As noted, professional magicians may use cold reading techniques when they try to mimic a psychic reading during mentalism acts.

Typical cold reading lines are things like: "Sometimes you are the life of the party, but you also like to spend time alone with your own thoughts." "You sometimes have a pain in one of your joints or limbs." "I feel that you have been thinking about an old relationship recently." "People don't appreciate just how much effort you put into your work." These lines can apply to anyone.

"Hot" Readings

A "hot" reading is where a "psychic" discovers specific information about a person and then recites it back to them during the "reading." One famous "psychic" had his assistants go into the crowd attending his show, and talk to the attendees. Then his assistants would tell him what the attendees had told them.

Later, during the show, he would call upon the people whom his assistants had secretly interviewed, and he would *amazingly* know the information that they had revealed to his assistants.

"Warm" Readings

A psychic does a "warm" reading when they take non-psychic information about the client and then relate it back to them as information that was received psychically.

For example, a client comes in with shoddy clothes, no jewelry, and other appearances of poverty. The psychic says, "I sense that your question today is about money."

That's not being psychic. That's doing a "warm" reading.

Even genuine psychics can fall into the warm reading trap, though, if, during the reading, they ask a client something like, "Is this making sense to you?" and then either proceed with the reading as it's going or change what they are saying based upon the client's response.

If we are truly getting our information from a psychic or spiritual source, then we should *not* look to the client for confirmation or validation as to what we are saying. We should first simply obtain and relate the information that we get from our psychic or spiritual source, and only <u>after that</u> should we discuss it with the client and attempt to interpret it.

Otherwise, we run the risk of unintentionally doing a "warm" reading, which can be a breach of our ethics and a disservice to our clients and ourselves.

Chapter 15: Determining Your Own Code Of Ethics

For you to determine your own personal code of ethics, the following questions are presented for your consideration.

Note that, while there may be no ethically "right" or "wrong" answers to some questions, there may be legally "right" or "wrong" answers, depending upon your local laws.

Advertising

*   Is it ethical to advertise your services?

*   Is it ethical to overstate your qualifications or achievements?

*   Is it ethical to overstate the benefits that clients (by "client" I mean anyone you give a reading to) might receive from your services?

*   Is it ethical to overstate the results that others have received from your services?

Initial Interview

*   Is it ethical for you to hold back information about yourself that might dissuade the client from engaging your services?

*   Is it ethical for you to exaggerate information about yourself that might encourage a client to engage your services?

Fees

*   Is it ethical to charge a fee for your services?

*   Is it ethical to have hidden extra charges or "up-sells"?

*   When is it ethically best for you to inform a client about the fees for your services?

Your Own Wellness/Competence

*   Is it ethical for you to perform your services when you are not feeling 100%?

*   Is it ethical if the client knows you are not feeling 100% but wants your services anyway?

*   Could it ever be ethical for you to perform services that you don't feel 100% competent to do but the client wants you to do it anyway?

*   Is it ethical for you to not always inform your clients of the limits of your abilities?

Professional Advice

*   Is it ethical - or even legal - for you to provide medical, financial, or legal advice?

*   If you refer clients to other professionals, is it ethical to make those referrals based on referral fees you might receive as compared to the services that the client might actually need?

Confidentiality

* Is it ever ethical for you to reveal confidential client information?
    - When seeking further guidance from a more experienced counselor?
    - For an article or book that might make you some money?
    - If the client revealed a criminal act or intent?

Are there times when you <u>should</u> breach a client's confidentiality?

Sexual Conduct

* Is it ever ethical for a practitioner to engage in sexual conduct with a client, either inside or outside of the practitioner-client relationship?
* How should we ethically handle a situation where a client is personally attracted to us?

Aggressive Conduct

* Is it ever ethical for you to engage in aggressive conduct, such as being overbearing, harassing, intimidating, demanding, bullying, nagging, or offensive?
* Is it ever ethical for you to refuse to allow others, including clients, to have their own thoughts, feelings, interpretations, opinions, values, or attitudes?

*   Is it ethical for you to demand that others, including clients, admit that you are correct?

The Four Ds
*   Is it ethical to make predictions that include the "Four Ds": death, divorce, disaster or disease?
*   On the other hand, is it ethical to withhold negative information that you might get during a reading?

Failures to Connect/Differences in Opinion
*   If you feel that there is a big difference in worldviews between you and the client (for example, you believe everything is guided by angels, and they don't), should you proceed with the session?
*   If you feel that there is a personality conflict between you and the client, should you proceed with the session?
*   If you feel that there is a failure on all levels to connect between you and the client, should you proceed with the session?
*   How can we ethically handle a client who won't take responsibility for their life or wants to play the "victim"?

Other Practitioner-Client Relationship Issues
*   Is the client inferior to the practitioner?
*   Is it ethical to feel superior to the client?

*   Do we need to "prove" our abilities or impress our clients through our readings or healings?

*   Is it ethical to develop an emotional investment in your clients?

*   What can we ethically do if we are repulsed or offended by a client's intentions or desires?

*   What are your obligations to your clients?

*   What do you <u>not</u> owe to your clients?

<u>Other Session Limits</u>

*   Is it ethical to conduct sessions for persons under the age of 18?

*   Is it ethical to conduct sessions for persons with mental/intellectual challenges?

*   Is it ethical to conduct sessions for people who seem to be addicted to sessions, or to us personally?

<u>Other People</u>

*   Is it ethical to spy on or "tune in" to other people to answer a client's question?

*   Is it ethical to reveal private information that you learn during a psychic reading about a third party?

*   Could it ever be ethical to send healing energies to someone without their consent or knowledge?

*   Could it ever be ethical to attempt to influence or manipulate third parties without their consent or knowledge?

<u>Yourself and Your Ethics</u>
*   Is it OK to provide readings or healings that compromise you in some way?
*   Can something be unlawful but still be ethical?
*   How can we protect against situations that test our ethics?
*   When you create a code of ethics, who is it meant to protect - yourself, the client, or the code of ethics itself?

As I said above, these are just a few of questions that we need to decide for ourselves in determining our own code of ethics when we are providing psychic counseling services. In your practice, other questions may come up.

Hopefully, your review of this section will at least give you a foundation from which you can decide whether other situations might or might not break your ethics.

So please consider these questions carefully, and answer them honestly to yourself, and then build your practice based upon your responses. And then be able to look yourself in the mirror each and every day and be proud of and love the person that you see. That's what really counts.

Chapter 16: Creating A Safe Space For Readings

Some people who embark on the path of psychic development have concerns about having negative experiences or encountering dark energies.

I have found that keeping a positive, loving intention with my focus always on the light goes a long way towards keeping me spiritually protected – for light naturally attracts light.

There are additional things we can do towards creating and maintaining a safe place for psychic/spiritual work.

Many people say a prayer or invocation before doing a reading or using a space for psychic or spiritual work.

Another technique is called "smudging," which involves using smoke from a bundle of sage, cedar, or sweetgrass to clear away any negative energies from an area.

Negative energies can also be cleared from an area by the use of certain sounds. Bells, cymbals (such as tingsha), gongs, and "singing bowls" can all be good for this.

You can also use crystals to clear away negative energies and bring in positive energies.

Purple amethyst brings spiritual energy and eliminates negative energy. Rose quartz brings love energy. Clear quartz, especially "Herkimer diamond," increases psychic ability and brings clarity and focus.

I keep all three near me most of the time, either in a bag, in my pocket or as part of a necklace, and I put them out on my table when doing a reading.

Another easy way of creating a safe space using crystals is called "gridding". Gridding can be done on a small area in a room, but can also be used on larger spaces, such as entire buildings.

Just set three crystals (rose or clear quartz are commonly used) in a triangle that encloses the area that you want to protect.

So if you're doing a reading at a particular table in a room you could set the three crystals so that they created a triangle that included the reading table area. Or if you wanted to protect an entire building you would put the three crystals outside of the building in a triangle that included the building.

When you place crystals outside it's OK to bury them slightly in the dirt to protect them from being accidentally displaced by animals, rain, or anything else.

The most important part of the process is setting your intent that the placement of the crystals will protect the space from any negative energies. so it's very important to stay focused while you are placing the crystals.

Chapter 17: Becoming A Clear Channel

When working to get psychic information, it's important to do our best to be a "clear channel" and not be distracted by sympathy, empathy or pity for the situation or any other person.

Ralph Jordan discusses this dynamic in detail in his book "The Psychic Counselor's Handbook" (Inner Perceptions, 1999).

In brief, while the personal situations of people who come to us for psychic guidance may excite our sympathy, empathy or pity, the truth is that when we get emotionally involved then it can interfere with our ability to receive psychic guidance clearly. Only by keeping our own feelings out of the picture can we truly be able to receive clear and untainted psychic information that will be accurate and useful for the other person.

Many people find it useful to recite an invocation before doing a reading or trying to obtain psychic information, to help ensure the clarity of the guidance received, such as: "I invoke the Light of Spiritual Wisdom and I open to the Light" or "I am a clear and perfect channel for the light of psychic wisdom."

Whether you find these invocations useful, or prefer to develop one of your own, it is important to recognize that our own feelings and associations may "taint" a reading, and that positive steps taken towards reducing such a taint may help us more clearly receive accurate information.

Chapter 18: Creating Well-Formed Questions

"'Would you tell me, please, which way I ought to go from here?' asked Alice.
'That depends a good deal on where you want to get to,' said the Cheshire Cat."
~ Lewis Carroll, *"Alice's Adventures in Wonderland"*

Alice did not ask a well-formed question.

Another person who failed to ask a well-formed question was King Croesus of Lydia in about 547 B.C. He asked the Oracle at Delphi if he should attack the Persians, who lived across the Halys river.

The Oracle replied: "If Croesus crosses the Halys, he will destroy a great empire." Based on this response, Croesus did attack the Persians. But the empire destroyed was his own when he lost the battle.

If our questions are not specific and clear, the answers may not be either. To get clear responses to psychic questions we need to be able to create clear, well-formed questions.

Often, people pose questions such as: "When will I meet Mr. Right?" or "Will I be rich?"

The right-brain psychic mind takes things very literally, almost like a computer. It doesn't easily process a question like: "Will I be rich?" Rich in what? Compared to what? When are you referring to? Tomorrow? Ten years from now?

Your questions must be very precise and easy to understand. If you get a vague or unclear response, try refining or rephrasing your question in a way that a computer would understand.

Here are six guidelines for creating well-formed questions:

Questions Should Be Specific

Asking "Will it rain tonight?" would be unspecific - after all, it's always raining somewhere, right? Instead, ask "Will it rain here tonight?"

In formulating your questions, be as specific as possible as to who, what, where, and when.

You are seeking a piece to a puzzle. As much as you can, specify your question so that only the missing piece is in question.

Generally, stay away from uncertain words such as "could", "should", "can", "try", "what if", "might", and so forth. This is most important when you are working to obtain psychic information for another person, as during a reading.

For example, perhaps John's wallet is missing. "Is John's wallet in his bedroom?" is a clear, well-framed question. "Should we try looking in the bedroom for John's missing wallet?" is really horrible, and will probably result in all kinds of vague and incomprehensible responses.

Keep in mind that we are already working in a (compared to the physical world) somewhat uncertain environment when we seek psychic guidance.

Our paths can be littered with "red herrings" generated by memories, associations, emotional blocks, fears, etc. To really obtain clear guidance, you must be sure that your question is as clear and specific as possible.

Questions Should Be Set In The Present, Or Be Time-Specific

The psychic mind is naturally always in the present, and so any questions regarding past or future dates must be very specific. "Someday", "soon", "in the future", et cetera, are vague and meaningless to the subconscious.

All that the psychic mind knows is that we're not talking about _now_. If we want to address something in the future or the past, it must be specific: "This Wednesday", "on July 4th", "yesterday", or even "the next time that you notice an attractive stranger".

These are time-specific.

Questions Should Avoid Non-Concrete Terms

The importance of being specific applies to your use of non-concrete terms in your questions as well. "Non-concrete terms" are words or phrases that mean something different to different people, and would include words like "love", "success", "rich", "relationship", "good", "better" or "best", and so forth.

"Will my relationship with John turn into love?" might get a clear "yes" answer, but the truth could be that he loves you like a sister, and has no romantic interest in you.

"Will I be happy if I take the new job offer?" might get a definite "no", but the unhappiness might be because of strained relationships with your family or friends who resent the demands of your new duties, and not be related to the environment at the job itself at all.

Questions Should Be Framed In The Positive

We need to keep in mind that the right-brain psychic mind doesn't process negatives. For example, if someone says "Don't think of a pink elephant", the first thing that the mind does is to think of a pink elephant.

In psychic work, likewise keep your questions to the subconscious in the positive. "Will I marry John?" - not "Won't I ever marry John?" "Will I get a raise in salary this year?" - not "Won't I ever get a raise?"

Questions Should Not Be Compound

Also avoid compound questions - questions that incorporate two or more questions. "Will I win the lottery and live a care-free life on a Greek island?" might get a "no" answer, and so you might fail to buy that winning lottery ticket next week, but only because you were going to change your mind and use the money instead to buy an apartment in Paris and decide to live the "care-free" life there!

Compound questions will commonly get a "no" or an unclear response, because they require that all parts of the question be true to get a clear "yes."

It's better to break up the question into parts and ask each one separately, so that you can get a clear response to each part.

Questions Should Not Include Presuppositions

A presupposition supposes or assumes a preceding condition or act, and is therefore similar to a compound question.

For example, "Will I get a phone call from John after dinner tonight?" presupposes you're going to have dinner tonight.

If something will happen to prevent you from having dinner, then the question will get a "no" answer, even if John is going to end up calling you 17 times later on this evening.

So to sum up: a clear, well-formed question for getting the clearest psychic guidance is one that is:

* Specific as to what information is sought, people, places, etc.

* In the present tense, or very specific as to any other time
* Does not include non-concrete terms
* Framed in the positive
* Not compound
* Does not include presuppositions

Unfortunately, the friends and clients that come to us for readings don't know anything about using clear questions to get clear answers.

It is not unusual for psychics to hear questions like: "Hey, I just met this guy Joe and we seemed to hit it off pretty well. Should I get into a relationship with him?" or "I heard about this job that's opening in a nearby town. Should I take it?"

There are a couple ways to deal with these kinds of questions.

You can ask the client/friend for more clarification: "'Should you get into a relationship with Joe?' What would you hope to get from the relationship? Some fun dates, or perhaps something more serious?" or " 'Should you take the new job?' What aspects of the new job would make it worth taking or not? More money? More opportunity? Is it a good career move?"

Another thing you can do is simply rephrase their question so that it is clearer and better formed, and then use the clearer question as the basis for the reading.

I've heard a million "should I" questions, and in time you probably will, too.

But "should" means something different to us than it does to our clients, because they know the criteria for deciding whether they "should" do this or "should" do that, and we don't know that criteria.

So we can't just answer a "should I" question directly. We need to use better questions.

Remember, clear questions for clear answers! Please stay true to this formula. It works!

Chapter 19: Ten Potential Causes for Errors in Readings

There will be times when your readings are not 100% accurate. Don't let it overwhelm you when it happens. It happens to all of us, once in a while.

Over time, though, I have found that there are ten common reasons for readings going wrong.

Try to avoid these, and your accuracy in readings should be much better.

1.   The reading wasn't based on a clear, well-formed question.

We went over this in pretty good detail in the last section, so you should understand the dynamics of this issue. The simpler and clearer the question, then the simpler and clearer the psychic responses will be. If people only asked us yes-or-no questions we could probably go all day and be spot-on 99% of the time.

2.   Sympathy/empathy/pity influencing the results (not being a clear channel).

When I do a reading for someone, I generally want to be told as little as possible at the beginning - just enough to be able to create clear questions and jump right into it.

We're all human, and it is very easy to get emotionally involved in other people's stories, and to hope that they get a favorable reading, but we aren't doing them any favors if we allow our feelings to interfere with their reading.

While you're doing the reading, you must let go of things like feelings of empathy for the client. This isn't being cold-hearted - it's doing your professional best to give the client the best reading that you can.

I bought my first Tarot deck when I was a kid back in the 1970's, and when I started giving readings to my friends everybody liked getting readings from me because my readings were always so positive. Yay! Everybody gets good readings!

What I didn't realize was that my great desire to make people happy and give readings that they enjoyed was resulting in me influencing the cards, so that they always came out positive.

If all we want to do is give positive readings, it's very easy - just take all the bad cards out of the Tarot deck. You'll never give a negative reading again.

But if you really want to give true and accurate readings from your psychic source, you must understand that sometimes the news may not be what the client wants to hear.

3. Interpreting before the guidance is fully revealed, overeagerness, and similar interpretation errors.

When we begin getting psychic information during a reading, our brain's first reaction will be to try to interpret the information and give it context so that we can understand it. But that may interfere with the accuracy of the guidance we receive.

For example, during a reading, I may receive an image that appears to be red spokes radiating out from a hub on a white background. In my own mind, I may try to interpret that image as a wheel, and say, "oh, I'm getting a vision of a wheel."

But if I relay the information exactly as received to my client, she may respond, "Oh, that's clearly an image of the flag of Japan - and that has very significant importance to me. I'm going there next month."

The way to avoid this error is to finish the reading before you begin any interpretation of the results, and to only report to the client the exact responses that you got without interpreting.

Then, <u>afterward</u>, the two of you can work together on the interpreting.

4.   Misinterpreting results because we think that the true results "don't make sense."

Sometimes the meaning of the information that we get in a psychic reading is not always immediately obvious. That's OK. It happens often.

Of course, discuss the information that you get in full with the client, so you can get their input and they can get your input, and make notes about everything.

As noted above, what may not be clear to you may be very clear to them.

But if, at the end, the two of you have not come to a full understanding of the meaning of the information, then you both should just take a break for a few days before coming back to it.

In these cases, which are actually pretty rare, my experience is that when the reader and the client talk about it again a few days later things have become much clearer, and most of the time the meaning of the reading has become clear.

5.	Performance anxiety interfering with being a clear channel.

Almost every professional psychic, when they first got started, had thoughts like, "I don't know what I'm doing. I'm not any good at this. I'm a fake. I'm a failure." This is *very* common.

You must reject these thoughts, or they will become a self-fulfilling prophecy. If you have developed your psychic abilities, and mastered your tools, then *trust in that*. Don't let negativity or self-doubt destroy the wonderful work you can do.

6.	Distraction by one piece of the picture.

Another potential cause for people thinking that there was an error in the reading can occur if people become too focused on one aspect of the reading, and disregard other aspects or the "big picture" view of the reading.

Again, the solution is to finish the reading before doing any interpreting, and not to let any one aspect of the reading take too much dominance over the others. All of the psychic guidance that you receive is important. Don't let any of it be discounted.

7.   A lack of intent being set.

I can't tell you how often people have told me, "I hear that you're good. Just deal the cards and let's see what you get."

That's not how it works, folks.

In order to get a psychic answer there must be a particular question. *We must always set a specific intent for a reading.*

Experienced psychics know to avoid these readings. Never let someone pressure you into giving a reading where no intent for the reading has been set and you'll be OK on this one.

8.   The effects of free will.

Readings are not set in stone. They simply indicate the result that will occur if the energies currently in effect don't change. If those energies *do* change, then *of course* the results will not be the same. That's not a failure, it's a success!

9.   Time-shifting or the reading is for yourself or another.

I was leading a telepathy class one time, in which I would look at a picture and mentally try to "send" the picture to the students and they would try to "receive" it. On one of the pictures a student got a whole bunch of vivid and distinct imagery that she described in great detail.

Unfortunately, it was all wrong. She was very disappointed and dejected. It had all seemed so clear!

But when I pulled the next picture out of the file for the next round, I had to stop and laugh - it was *exactly* the picture that she had described! Somehow she had time-shifted into the future just a bit, and seen a picture that I had not even sent yet!

I haven't run across that happening often, but it is possible. Likewise, a friend of mine told me about a psychic fair that she was working and all the readings were off sequence. The psychic guidance that she got for client #1 was actually for client #2, the guidance for client #2 was actually for client #3, and so forth.

We can also get guidance in a reading for someone else that is actually meant for us. If this starts happening to you, you will notice it. The way to solve it is to stop doing readings for other people for a moment and do some for yourself, so that the underlying issues can be resolved. Then you can move forward again.

10. The "error" is a false report - there really was no error.

This is very annoying when it happens, and I hope it doesn't happen to you, but it has happened to me and other readers that I know, so you should just be aware.

A person you gave a reading to may say something like, "I got a reading from you and it was all wrong." And you think, "oh my gosh, how embarrassing, I really messed up, etc." And then later on you find out that the reading in fact was *not* wrong, but that the person just decided to say it was for some personal reason.

Maybe they're angling for a refund, maybe they don't like the fact that you were right, maybe they just decided that they don't like your face. Whatever. It can happen, so just be aware that it can happen, and, again, don't let these things influence your self esteem, because all that will do is possibly negatively affect the next reading that you do. Stay clear, stay strong, and move on.

Section II

Psychic Reading

Methods, Oracles & Tools

Chapter 20: Methods, Oracles & Tools: An Overview

Since the beginning of recorded time, mankind has developed hundreds of ways to attempt to obtain information psychically or from gods, angels, oracles, or other metaphysical sources. Some of these sources, such as the Pythia, the famous Oracle at the Temple of Apollo at Delphi, are no longer around.

However, there is still a wide selection of great methods for doing readings. In this part of the book, we'll review some of the most popular methods in use today.

Like most people, you will probably find yourself more attracted to some of the methods and less drawn to others. That's perfectly fine. Just follow your gut instinct and you'll find the right method for you.

The methods reviewed in this section are:

* Cartomancy refers to obtaining guidance through the use of cards, including Tarot, Angel, or other specialized decks.

* Runes are another ancient method for obtaining guidance through the use of specially marked stones or markers.

* Pendulums and dowsing rods have been used for centuries in various cultures to find water, determine the sex of unborn babies, and many other things.

* Scrying is the art of obtaining visions from the inner mind by using crystal balls, black mirrors, or similar devices.

* Some readers obtain psychic guidance by watching for signs and omens, another ancient art.

* Automatic writing is a method of getting guidance by allowing the psychic mind to do the writing.

* Psychometry is used to get psychic information by holding or touching an object connected to the person or their question.

* Aura reading refers to discovering information about a person by what the psychic observes in the person's aura, the energy field that fills and surrounds our physical bodies.

* Direct psychic guidance means simply obtaining guidance in the mind directly through psychic awareness.

* Consulting higher self, spirit guides and angels.

Everyone has their favorite and least favorite methods, but try different methods out and give them a chance. I was always the "crystal guy" and I wasn't very fond of Tarot for decades until I found my perfect deck – which I loved! And once that door opened for me I have found many more decks that I can connect with as well.

Try several methods and figure out which ones you like best. While some psychics stick to a single method for readings, such as reading Tarot cards, many psychics will use two or more methods in a single reading.

Chapter 21: Cartomancy

Card reading is easily the most popular way that people give psychic readings these days.

Beside all of the various Tarot decks, there are hundreds of other decks available, including Angel cards, Power Animal cards, Fairy cards, Goddess cards, Shaman cards, and many, many more, as well as regular playing cards, and many ways to use them to perform readings.

A Tarot card deck normally consists of a deck similar to the standard 52 playing card deck, plus an additional face card, usually called the "Page" (with the standard "Jack" often being designated as the "Knight") and 22 "Major Arcana" cards.

The suits in a Tarot deck are commonly designated swords (corresponding to spades), cups (corresponding to hearts), wands or staves (corresponding to clubs), and pentacles or coins (corresponding to diamonds).

The suit cards, consisting of "pip" and "face" cards, are referred to as the "Minor Arcana." "Arcana" is a Latin word meaning "secrets."

There are many ways to use cards for readings. Sometimes, a single card is chosen, and the meaning of the card given as the answer to the person's question. Or three cards may be chosen, representing the past, present and future. Or a more detailed reading may be obtained by using a larger number of cards, such as in the popular "Celtic Cross" reading described below.

Some readers only use the Major Arcana cards for a short reading of one or more cards, while using the entire deck for a longer reading.

The Major Arcana

The Major Arcana cards are usually numbered 0 through 21, and are often depicted containing various symbols, such as may be found in astrology or the Kabbalah, and generally represent the person getting the reading (sometimes referred to as the "querent," which comes from the ancient Latin for "one who seeks"), and their journey through life or a new project.

The meanings of the cards discussed below *are* common but *are not* controlling. There are often big differences in the books or pamphlets that are generally enclosed with each set of cards.

In addition, hundreds of books and articles have been written exploring potential meanings and symbolism of the cards, including the meanings of cards being "reversed" (appearing upside down in a reading).

Further, many readers totally skip the "book meanings" of the cards and just let their psychic awareness guide them as to the meanings of the cards or the significance of their occurrence or placement in a particular reading.

The Major Arcana cards, along with their common meanings, are:

0 - The Fool: Often used as a representative card (or "significator") for the querent, the "Fool" is not a stupid person, but rather a naïve or uninformed free-spirited adventurer. He does not suspect the challenges that may lie ahead. Appearing in a reading, this card may indicate a new beginning or opportunity.

1 - The Magician: Male energy, mastery, inner talent, influence, doing.

2 - The High Priestess: Female energy, wisdom, nurturing, intuition, instincts, feeling.

3 - The Empress: Mother, fertility, creativity, security.

4 - The Emperor: Father, authority, power, logic, decisiveness.

5 - The Hierophant: Teacher, formal education, mentor, advisor, traditions and faith.

6 - The Lovers: The union of opposites, romance, partnerships, adolescence.

7 - The Chariot: Accomplishment, confidence, triumph.

8 - Strength: Energy, passion, self-respect, self-control.

9 - The Hermit: Planning, evaluating, wisdom, spiritual development, inner peace.

10 - Wheel of Fortune: A new cycle, influence of chance, advancement, rewards, progress, the ups and downs of life.

11 - Justice: A fair decision, balance, insight, harmony.

12 - The Hanged or Hanging Man: Stagnation, isolation, accepting the present, a new perspective.

13 - Death: Major change, transformation, liberation, renewal, an ending, death of the ego and self-delusion.

14 - Temperance: Moderation, emotional balance, compromise, avoid extremes, tolerance.

15 - The Devil: Material world desires, prejudice, abuse, our dark side.

16 - The Tower: Change, re-structuring, spiritual awakening, self-improvement, change in beliefs.

17 - The Star: Hope, inspiration, optimism, healing, discovery, guidance.

18 - The Moon: The subconscious, dreams, intuition, imagination, but have a care for the shadows.

19 - The Sun: Success, self-awareness, good health, warmth, joy of living, reward, achievement.

20 - Judgment: Understanding, forgiveness, acceptance of past, new perception.

21 - The World: Overcoming challenges, experience, fulfillment, end of a cycle, wholeness.

The Minor Arcana

The Minor Arcana cards commonly include four face cards and ten numbered cards in each of four suits: wands (or staves), cups, swords, and pentacles (or coins).

The various suits represent individual energies or dynamics in life:

Wands: Represent spirituality. Their element is fire. Wand cards often indicate inspiration, projects, or career.

Cups: Represent emotions. Their element is water. Cup cards in a reading may relate to relationships or creativity.

Swords: Represent thought or mental activity. The element of Swords is air. Sword cards occurring in a reading may represent challenges through differing or changing perspectives.

Pentacles: Represent the material world. Their element is earth. Pentacle cards usually indicate activities regarding money or other earthly resources.

The "face" or "court" cards are generally interpreted as follows:

Page: May refer to a young person, a girl, or a novice. Symbolically, the page may indicate a new situation, project, or a message.

Knight: May be a teen, young adult, or a boy, or the Knight can also symbolize a fast-moving situation.

Queen: Generally represents an adult woman who is involved in or has an influence upon the situation in question in the reading. If the querent is a woman the card may also represent her or her role.

King: Usually represents an adult man involved or influential in the subject situation, or may represent the querent if a man.

Numbered or "Pip" Cards. The very general meanings given below may relate to the significance of a particular card as it appears <u>within the context of its suit and position in the reading layout</u>.

For example, while aces generally reflect a new beginning or opportunity, an ace of swords may represent a new idea, an ace of cups a new relationship, an ace of wands a new project, and an ace of pentacles a new income source or financial opportunity.

An ace in a position revealing the past may show a missed opportunity, in a position of the present it may represent a current opportunity, and in a position of the future it may represent an opportunity yet to come.

Ace - New beginnings, opportunity.
Two - Balance, duality, connection, a crossroads or choice.
Three - Achievement, resolution.
Four - Structure, stability, perhaps stagnation.

Five - Change, challenge, instability, perhaps conflict or loss.

Six - Communication, problem-solving, cooperation, overcoming a challenge.

Seven - Reflection, assessment, inner growth.

Eight - Power, movement, action, success.

Nine - Fruition, attainment, satisfaction.

Ten - Completion, end of a cycle, a coming change.

Preparing The Cards For A Reading

Readers differ on how they prefer to have the cards prepared for a reading. Some readers have the querent shuffle or cut the cards while focusing on their question, and then the reader takes the deck and just deals off the top.

I spread out all the cards in a big mess face down and then ask my psychic guidance to be visually attracted to cards that will be relevant to the reading. Experiment with different methods and then choose the one that feels the most comfortable to you.

Some readers also remove certain cards from the deck before doing a reading, in the belief that those cards may be too distressing or misleading to the querent.

Cards removed may include Death, the Hanged Man, the Devil, and the Tower. For me, these cards don't necessarily indicate real "disasters," and I leave them in the deck for my readings.

Draws And Spreads

A "draw" is when one or more cards are drawn from a deck for a reading. A fast and easy way to do a Tarot reading is to decide on a question and then draw one card from the deck as the answer. Doing a lot of one card draws is a great way to get to know a deck.

A "spread" is the way that the cards are arranged for a reading. For example, a reading of the past, present and future of a situation might consist of a "spread" of three cards in a row, with the leftmost card representing the past, the center card representing the present, and the rightmost card representing the future.

How many cards should you use for a certain reading? What spread should be used?

These are very important questions, but their resolution hinges strongly on how well you know your deck and how the cards interact with you and each other. Your skills in this area will develop the more you practice with the deck.

The Celtic Cross is one of the most popular Tarot card spreads used to do an in-depth reading on a particular question. This spread uses ten cards, plus a significator card to represent the querent. The Fool, a face card, or a card randomly drawn from the deck, may be used as a significator.

Place the significator card face up on the table. The next card is placed directly on top of the significator.

The Celtic Cross spread:

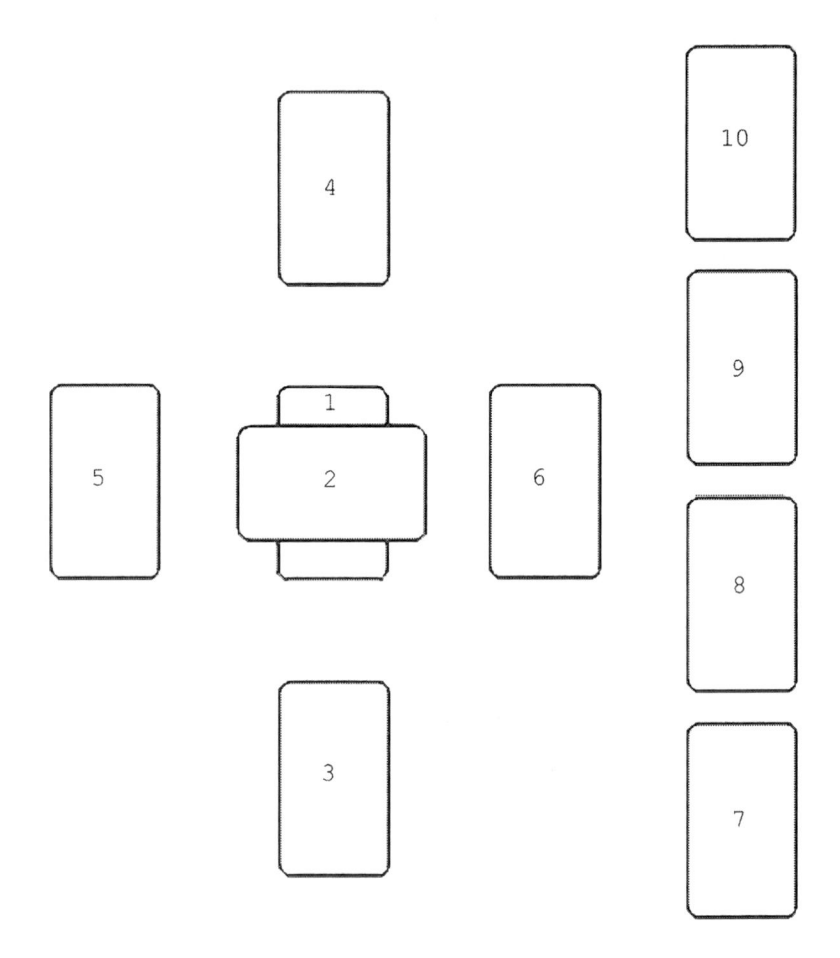

```
                    ┌─────┐                ┌─────┐
                    │     │                │     │
                    │  4  │                │ 10  │
                    │     │                │     │
                    └─────┘                └─────┘

                                           ┌─────┐
                                           │     │
                                           │  9  │
                                           │     │
                                           └─────┘
                      ┌─1─┐
┌─────┐           ┌───┴───┴───┐   ┌─────┐
│     │           │     2     │   │     │
│  5  │           │           │   │  6  │  ┌─────┐
│     │           └───┬───┬───┘   │     │  │     │
└─────┘               └───┘       └─────┘  │  8  │
                                           │     │
                                           └─────┘

                    ┌─────┐                ┌─────┐
                    │     │                │     │
                    │  3  │                │  7  │
                    │     │                │     │
                    └─────┘                └─────┘
```

Take the first card and place it on top of the significator card, saying, "This covers her." This card represents the general question or situation. (I'm using the word "her" here as a general pronoun for the querent. If the querent was a male, of course, you'd say "This covers him," and change the references below likewise.)

Take the second card and place it on top of the first card, but turned 90 degrees, saying, "This crosses her." This card shows the immediate challenge or obstacle facing the querent with respect to the situation.

Take the third card and place it on the table below the original pile of the significator, first and second cards, saying, "This is beneath her." This card indicates the foundation of the situation or question.

Take the fourth card and place it on the table above the original pile, saying, "This crowns her." This card represents the querent's goal or what the querent expects from the situation.

Take the fifth card and place it on the table to the left of the original pile, saying, "This is behind her." This card shows the recent past or a passing influence with regard to the situation.

Take the sixth card and place it on the table to the left of the original pile, saying, "This is before her." This card indicates the immediate future or a coming influence with regard to the situation.

At this point you should have the original pile of cards in the center with a circle of four cards around it.

Now you are going to make a row of cards to the right of the circle. This new row of cards is sometimes called the "staff," and the staff and circle together make the Celtic Cross.

Take the seventh card and place it to the right of the circle, saying, "How you are influencing the matter." This card represents the querent's influence on the situation.

Take the eighth card and place it above the seventh card, saying, "How others are influencing the matter." This card shows the influence of friends, family and others on the situation.

Take the ninth card and place it above the eighth card, saying, "Your hopes and fears." This card indicates the querent's hopes and fears regarding the situation. This is more emotionally based and thus different from the fourth card.

Finally, take the tenth card and place it above the ninth card, saying, "The final outcome." This card represents how the situation is currently likely to end up.

If the querent doesn't feel that she got enough information from the first reading then another reading may be done, this time using the tenth card - the final out come card from the first reading - as the new significator. This reading would essentially be a reading of that card, and thus can yield a great more detailed information regarding that one particular issue.

Sample Tarot Reading

A client (we'll call him Sam) at a psychic fair asked: How can I increase sales at my comic book store business?

Psychic fair readings are commonly set for short lengths of time, such as 10, 15 or 20 minutes, so long in-depth spreads with lots of cards usually aren't appropriate.

After invoking the light of psychic guidance, we decided to use five cards, representing various aspects of the situation: 1) the business as it was in the past, 2) the business as it is now, and 3, 4 and 5) three different ideas or energies that Sam could use to add to or change the business to increase the sales.

For this reading, I used Ciro Marchetti's *Gilded Tarot* deck.

The first card drawn was the four of wands.

The second card drawn was the six of cups.

The third card was the eight of pentacles, the fourth card was the queen of swords, and the fifth card was the nine of cups.

The first card drawn, the four of wands, which in this reading represented the business as it was in the past, shows a happy family inside a strong structure of found wands set firmly in the ground in a square and decorated with flowers. A dragonfly is flying by, and some rabbits are nibbling on the grass.

This card shows stability and harmony resulting from hard work. Sam has built a firm, strong foundation in his store.

The six of cups, representing the business as it is now, shows children playing amidst six cups full of flowers. A cat is in the foreground, looking at us.

The six of cups can represent happy memories of the past that are interfering with the querent's ability to move forward in the present. The querent needs to let go of the past in order to effectively deal with the situation as it is today.

The next three cards were drawn for ideas for three different ideas or energies that Sam could use to add to or change his business to increase the sales.

The first of these "idea" cards was the eight of pentacles. This card shows a young man working at his desk late into the night. The card is sometimes called the "apprenticeship card," and may indicate developing a new skill or a possible change in profession. I sometimes read this card as meaning "all work and no play makes Jack a dull boy," and that some balance between work life and personal time is needed.

The second "idea" card we drew was the queen of swords, which depicts a strong, attractive woman holding up a large sword. Bright light reflects from her crown. The card usually signifies a smart, independent woman, confident and fearless.

The final "idea" card drawn was the nine of cups. This card shows a smiling man, perhaps an inn or tavern-keeper, holding a cup aloft in celebration, with many other cups placed on barrels and the table around him. The nine of cups is a very positive card, indicating happiness and achievement of an important goal.

Sam generally agreed with the meanings of the first two cards, and he was ready to use the new ideas presented by the last three cards to get his business going strong again.

In order to get the most creative ideas from these cards, though, we ignored the typical meanings, and just did some free-form associating based on the images shown in the cards.

Sam thought that the hard-working fellow in the eight of pentacles could represent a comic book artist, and got the idea of having artists make special appearances at his store, to talk about their comic books and do signings and sell original artwork.

The image of the strong queen with her sword gave him the idea of adding action figures and models to his inventory.

The final "idea" card, the nine of cups, with its happy innkeeper, gave Sam the idea of turning a part of the store into a lounge section with a refreshment bar, to encourage customers to feel welcome to stay and hang out at the store. The store's income would also grow through the sale of drinks and snacks.

While the format that we chose was not a "traditional" Tarot reading, Sam was very satisfied, and I think it demonstrates just how versatile and powerful the Tarot can be.

The Tarot is much, much more than a stack of cardboard pieces with pictures on them. There are thousands upon thousands of stories that it has to tell. And each one can help you take another step towards complete psychic awareness.

Chapter 22: Runes

Runes, as defined by The World English Dictionary, are the characters of an ancient Germanic alphabet, derived from the Roman alphabet, in use, especially in Scandinavia, from the 3rd century A.D. to the end of the Middle Ages. Each character was believed to have a magical significance.

There are actually several different old Germanic alphabets that people use for rune readings, including the Elder Futhark, Gothic, and Younger Futhark. The Elder Futhark seems to be the most popular set in use today, and is shown along with the common rune meanings below.

For divination purposes, the runes are painted, carved, or otherwise inscribed on a set of stones, wooden or clay blocks, or something similar. To do a reading, you should ask your question and then blindly draw one or three (or however many you think is necessary) runes from a bag and then do your reading from those.

There are usually many sets of various runes available on popular websites like eBay or Amazon for under $20, or you can easily make a set of your own.

Runes are somewhat like Tarot cards in that the best way to get to know them is to just start working with them, doing readings for yourself or your friends. The more you use them the quicker you will master the art of reading them.

"The Runes have their own lives, they are true magical signs, from which we can draw the Spirit to Advise and the Courage to Action."
~ Rudolf John Gorsleben

The 24 Elder Futhark rune symbols, along with their names, basic meanings, and generally accepted interpretations, are given below. When doing readings, some readers will include reversed or "merkstave" interpretations, and others sometimes use a blank stone or marker as a "wild card."

The Elder Futhark Runes

ᚠ - Fehu: Cattle

ᚢ - Uruz: Aurochs (oxen)

ᚦ - Thurisaz: A giant

ᚨ - Ansuz: The god Odin

ᚱ - Raidho: Wagon or ride

ᚲ - Kenaz: Torch

ᚷ - Gebo: Gift

ᚹ - Wunjo: Joy

ᚺ - Hagalaz: Hail/hailstones

ᚾ - Nauthiz: Need/necessity

ᛁ - Isa: Ice

ᛃ - Jera: A year

ᛇ - Eihwaz: Yew tree

ᛈ - Perthro: Dice cup

ᛉ - Algiz: Elk

ᛋ - Sowilo: The sun

ᛏ - Tiwaz: The god Tyr

ᛒ - Berkano: Goddess of the birch

ᛖ - Ehwaz: Horse

ᛗ - Mannaz: Man, mankind

ᛚ - Laguz: Water

ᛜ - Ingwaz: The god Ing

ᛞ - Dagaz: Day or dawn

ᛟ - Othala: Ancestral home/property

Fehu (Cattle): Wealth, prosperity, issues regarding financial or material matters, coming abundance or success.

Uruz (Aurochs): Physical strength, energy, vitality, good health, action, sexuality/virility, or a positive change.

Thurisaz (A giant): Hardship, tough times, a cleansing, conflict, knowledge, or a difficult change or transformation.

Ansuz (Odin, the god of battle, victory, wisdom and prophecy, and the father of Thor): A leader, justice, prophetic awareness, wisdom, truth, or a sign, vision or message.

Raidho (Wagon or ride): Travel or a journey (figurative or literal), a pilgrimage, destiny, or a change.

Kenaz (Torch): Insight, revelation, wisdom, creativity, inspiration, passion, strength, power, or a solution to a challenge.

Gebo (Gift): Unexpected good fortune, an offering, a gift, an exchange, generosity, relationships, love or marriage.

Wunjo (Joy): Happiness, pleasure, harmony, success, reward, or achievement.

Hagalaz (Hail/hailstones): Disaster, loss, destruction, a sudden unexpected change, or a test or trial.

Nauthiz (A need or necessity): Poverty, patience, frustration, delay, discontent, facing your destiny.

Isa (Ice): Stagnation, frustration, a block or obstacle, patience, withdrawal, reflection or rest.

Jera (A year): The turning of the wheel of the year, a new cycle, a good harvest, expected change or growth, reward for good work done or an earned success.

Eihwaz (Yew tree): A turning point, a transformation, change, strength, endurance, overcoming fears, or achievement of goals.

Perthro (Dice cup): A mystery, something unknown or hidden, a new beginning (not necessarily expected), female energy, magic, or a prophecy.

Algiz (Elk): Protection, support, assistance, a strong defense, a warning, or a guardian or mentor.

Sowilo (The sun): Power, success, positive energy or changes, inner strength, or good health.

Tiwaz (Tyr, the god of the sky, law and justice): Doing one's duty, honor, justice, leadership, being true to yourself, or success.

Berkano (The goddess of the birch tree): Birth (literally or figuratively), fertility, new beginnings, renewal, or growth.

Ehwaz (Horse): Transportation, forward movement, energy, power, progress, harmony, or a good partnership or team.

Mannaz (Man, mankind): The self, family, community, relationships, social issues, intelligence, or skills/abilities.

Laguz (Water): Intuition, dreams, emotions, mysteries, energy or life flow, or the sea.

Inguz or Ingwaz (The god Ing): Work, production, male energy, being balanced/grounded, or family love.

Dagaz (Day or dawn): Happiness, success, awakening, awareness, personal transformation through clarity, or a new beginning.

Othala (Ancestral home or property): Home, inheritance, family homeland, heritage, or family values.

Sample Rune Reading

A client ("Nikki") asked, will I be married within a year?

Having first created a safe space, and invoked the light of psychic guidance, we drew three runes from the bag, to represent 1) the influence of internal forces, 2) the influence of external forces, and 3) the final result.

The runes drawn were 1) Eihwaz, the yew tree, 2) Gebo, a gift, and 3) Nauthiz, a need or necessity.

Eihwaz can indicate a turning point or a transformation. Nikki was coming up on 30 years of age, and she was feeling "done" with dating, and she wanted to settle down in a steady relationship. These were the internal forces at work.

Gebo, the gift rune, is a rune that speaks of relationships, love or marriage. Nikki had been dating a guy, Steve, but so far Steve hadn't shown an interest in getting more serious about their relationship. Nikki had also attracted the flirtatious attention of Colin, a man who worked at the same office that she does, but they haven't gone out together yet.

Nauthiz, the third rune that was drawn, points to frustration and delay. If things continued in the direction they were going, it didn't appear that wedding bells were in Nikki's near future.

Nikki asked to draw one more rune for further insight into the situation, and the rune Dagaz, which means "day" or "dawn" is drawn. Dagaz is a very positive rune, that points to a positive personal transformation through clarity, an awakening, or a new beginning.

    I told Nikki that the runes were saying that she needed to get clarity from Steve about his vision for the future of their relationship. That would likely result in a change in their relationship: either a transformation and an awakening of a deeper relationship between them if Steve was interested in getting serious, or perhaps a new beginning with Colin if Steve wasn't serious and it became time for Nikki to leave him behind.

Chapter 23: Dowsing With Pendulums, Sticks And Rods

Dowsing is a very ancient art, used in a variety of cultures and societies since the beginning of recorded history.

According to the dictionary, dowsing is "a form of divination involving a rod or wand, especially the art of finding underground supplies of water, ores, etc. Also called rhabdomancy."

Essentially, dowsing involves holding a dowsing tool in your hand, such as a Y-shaped forked stick, dowsing rods (sometimes called L-rods, because they're made of metal rods bent into an L-shape), or a pendulum, asking a question, and getting a response from the dowsing tool.

Dowsing is fairly simple and and easy skill to master, and doesn't need much special instruction or tools. but it can reveal some surprising secrets.

Pendulums

To make a pendulum, just putting a weight on a string will do fine. You don't really need a special crystal or anything, but you certainly can if you so desire.

Hold the end of the string between your thumb and your index finger and allow the pendulum to hang still. Ask the pendulum to show you the movement for "yes." Do not try to consciously move the pendulum, and just allow it to move on its own. After a moment or two, the pendulum should begin to move.

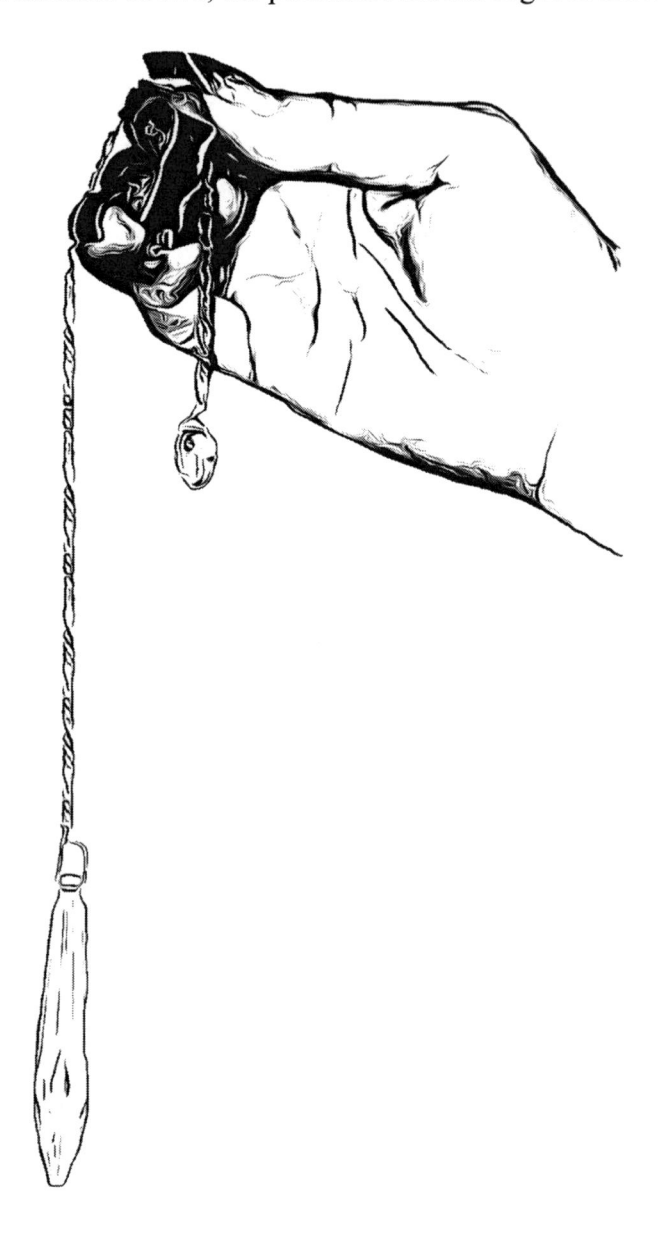

Be patient with it. (For me, the pendulum tends to start out by swinging around in a circle for a few moments, before giving me its definite "answer" swinging movement.) Then stop the pendulum and ask it for the movement for "no." After you've done that, ask it for the movement for "unknown" or "maybe/maybe not," the movement that the pendulum should show you when the answer to the question is not known or set.

Once you have established the "yes," "no," and "unknown" response movements, then you can begin asking your pendulum simple questions.

The more you practice with the pendulum the better you'll get with it, and the more complex questions you will be able to explore with it.

Pendulums have been used for determining the sex of unborn babies, which foods are best for someone to eat, if a certain business opportunity should be taken, and much more.

> "It's hard to believe something as simple as a weight on a string can work magic. A pendulum is a powerful tool, yet small enough to carry around and use anytime. With just a few minutes of practice, anyone can start using it."
> *~ Richard Webster, author, "Pendulum Magic for Beginners: Tap Into Your Inner Wisdom"*

Y-Shaped Stick or L-Shaped Rods

People usually use the Y-shaped forked stick to find things, like underground water or a missing item. You hold the two ends of the "Y" loosely in your left and right hands, with the bottom end of the "Y" pointing in front of you.

Ask it to show you the item that you want to find, and start walking around the area where you think the item might be. When you come close to the item, the the bottom end of the stick should move in a definitive way.

Not everyone is able to do this kind of dowsing, but for those who can it can be a very exciting experience, as the stick sometimes seem to have a mind of its own and almost jumps out of your hands when you come upon the location of the item.

You can buy a professionally made set of the L-shaped dowsing rods, or just make them yourself from firm metal wire, like from a clotheshanger. Just bend them into an L-shape. You hold the short ends of the rods in your hands, with the long ends pointing in front of you. When you come upon the item you're searching for, the rods will move, either crossing over each other or moving apart. The best sets will have a handle on the short ends, so that the rods can swivel freely in your hands. You can make handles by wrapping aluminum foil loosely around the short ends.

You can find a lot more great information on dowsing at the website for the American Society of Dowsers at www.dowsers.org.

Sample Pendulum Reading

My friend Lizzie thought that her house might be haunted, and had asked me and some other friends to come check it out.

Before we all left my house to go over to Lizzie's house, though, I suggested that we do a pendulum reading, so that we might better know what we might encounter.

We created a safe space using crystals and invoked the light of psychic guidance, and asked some simple yes/no questions:

Is there a spiritual entity at Lizzie's house now? *Yes*

Does this spirit have a family relation to any of the people living at the house? *No*

Was the spirit at the house before Lizzie's family moved there? *Yes*

Is the spirit angry that Lizzie's family is there? *No*

Has the spirit been at the house for 30 years? *No*

Has the spirit been at the house for 20 years? *Yes*

Did the spirit live at that house as a human? *Yes*

Did that person die at the house? *Yes*

Did that person die violently? *No*

Did that person die of old age? *No*

Did that person die of illness? *Yes*

Was that person a male? *No*

Was that person a female? *Yes*

Was the person older than 10 years when she died? *Yes*

Was the person older than 20 years when she died? *Yes*

Was the person older than 30 years when she died? *Yes*

Was the person older than 40 years when she died? *Yes*

Was the person older than 50 years when she died? *Yes*

Was the person older than 60 years when she died? *No*

Was the person older than 55 years when she died? *Yes*

Does the spiritual entity want to stay at the house? *Yes*

Is the spirit emotionally attached to the house? *Yes*

Is the spirit lonely? *Yes*

Does the spirit miss her family? *Yes*

Is the spirit afraid to leave the house? *Yes*

This gave us a lot of basic material to work with when we went over to Lizzie's house. We knew that the house was indeed haunted, and that the spirit haunting the house had been there at least 20 years, and was a female who had once lived at the house but had died there of an illness in her late fifties.

The spirit missed her family and friends, but was afraid to leave the house for the spirit world.

Cases like this are very sad, but not uncommon. Not everyone transitions to the spirit world easily after death. In this situation, when we went to Lizzie's house, we did not make contact with the spirit immediately. But over the course of the next few days we were eventually able to communicate with the spirit and help her transition into the light of the spirit world.

Chapter 24: Scrying

Scrying refers to using a medium, such as a crystal, a black mirror, still water in a bowl or lake, clouds, sand, or other similar item to stimulate clairvoyant visions.

Scrying has been recorded as having been practiced in most cultures for thousands of years. Some of the best known scryers were Nostradamus (1503-1566), who used a bowl of water, John Dee (1527-1609), who used a black mirror, and Jeane Dixon (1904-1997), who used a crystal ball.

There are two basic methods to scry to get the answer to a question.

The first method is to gaze into a clear item, such as a crystal ball, or an item with an undisturbed surface, like a black mirror. In this kind of scrying, the reader at first usually sees nothing, and then sort of a white or gray "cloud," and then suddenly images will appear. The images, which can be static pictures or movies, are generally symbolic and the symbolism must be interpreted in order to divine the answer to the question.

The second method is to look at a medium that has a lot of random shapes in it, such as tea leaves, smoke smudges, or natural crystals, which are full of occlusions, inclusions, or other flaws. In this kind of scrying, the random shapes can act as kind of a Rorschach picture, and stimulate your psychic insights.

> "The mirror shows many things: things that were, things that are, and some things that have not yet come to pass."
> ~ *Galadriel (Cate Blanchett), in the movie "The Lord of the Rings: The Fellowship of the Ring"*

I would mention that I have run into a lot of superstition and misinformation in connection with scrying, particularly with regard to crystal balls, such as: scrying somehow can allow evil forces to get at you, the ball must be made of a certain material, only people of certain faiths can do scrying, scrying works best at some magical time of day or year, and so forth. *None of this stuff is true, so don't let it bother you.* Anybody can scry. The visions are all within you already. All that scrying does is provide a medium for those visions to manifest themselves clearly. I've had wonderful experiences scrying by simply gazing into a slow-moving stream.

To scry using the first method, think of a specific question, and then gaze into a clear crystal ball, a black mirror, a sand disk†, or other surface with no distracting flaws or reflections. When I use a crystal ball, I put a black cloth beneath the ball, darken the room entirely, and then set a candle about 12 inches to the side of the ball so that I can still see the ball but I avoid creating any direct reflection from the surface of the ball.

Stare into the center of the item and wait. After a while (perhaps 15-20 minutes when one is just beginning the practice), the center of the area being gazed into may become "cloudy." At some point afterward, a vision will suddenly appear in the "cloudy" area. Some people see static pictures, while others may see little "movies." These pictures or movies will generally be symbolic answers to your question.

While some people are able to see pictures or movies on the first try, most people need to practice it for a while first. So don't be disheartened if you don't see anything on your first attempt. It's very exciting when you start seeing things, so it's worth the effort!

To scry using the second method, again think of a specific question, and then look into a medium that has all kinds of random shapes in it, such as a cup with used tea leaves or a natural crystal with occlusions, inclusions, or other flaws. Notice if you see any "pictures" amongst the random shapes. If you do, these will be the images that you can interpret for the reading.

The second method is easier and quicker to get started with, because anyone can do it right away. But it will still take some practice to truly master the technique.

It may also take a little effort to find the medium that best works for you. For me, I find that my readings with crystals are much better than with tea leaves or smoke smudges, so I am always on the lookout for crystals that have lots of interesting internal flaws that can show me all kinds of pictures.

† A "sand disk" is a scrying tool that is easy and inexpensive to make yourself. Get a piece of scrap cardboard, wood, or a similar flat and firm material that is at least about six inches wide and long. It doesn't matter if it's round, square, or rectangular, as long as there is a good clear area about six inches square. Cover one side with a thin layer of craft glue. Then sprinkle fine sand over the glue and let it dry, then shake off the excess. Sand disks are easy to store or transport when necessary.

Sample Scrying Reading

For my readings, I do mostly either Tarot or scrying with crystals, so I do a lot of scrying, generally using the second method (seeing the pictures in the imperfections inside the crystals). I have about a dozen crystals that are full of hundreds of great possible pictures, and I usually use three or four of them during a reading. These kinds of readings are much easier to do at events like psychic fairs, because they don't require special settings, or a lot of time, or for me to go into a trance state. You just ask your question, look into the crystals, and see whatever it is that you see.

For this sample, I'll refer to a reading I did for a woman at a psychic fair. She was curious to discover if any romance was coming for her in the near future, and, if so, any details I could see.

I mentally posed the question, if there would be an opportunity for her to find love in the next four months, and I picked up one of the crystals and held it up to the light. (I usually see pictures easier if there is a good light behind the crystal.)

At first I saw a mountain, then a treasure chest, and then I actually saw an image of two people walking together.

I told her to write down the images as I saw them. When I do these kinds of readings I don't want to be distracted by having to look away from the crystal to write down what I see, but if we don't keep a record then things get forgotten, so I give the client the job of writing down whatever I see.

All three of these images were very positive to her question. A mountain to me means success, after some initial effort, but a treasure chest means abundance, and there was no need to interpret the two people walking together.

I then picked up another crystal and mentally posed the question: where can she find love in the next four months.

This time the images that I saw were: a flying bird, a large rock in a lake or other body of water, a group of three large trees, and a narrow walkway or bridge.

None of that made any sense to me, but she said that there was a popular restaurant/bar she liked called Seagull Rock, and that you approached it by a narrow walkway, so she was going to try hanging out there and see who she might meet. She actually met a guy there a few weeks later, and they started dating. *(But we never did figure out what the "three large trees" image meant.)*

Chapter 25: Signs And Omens

An omen is defined as anything perceived or happening that is believed to portend a good or evil event or circumstance in the future.

In some ancient cultures, before an important event (such as going to war) priests would sometimes slaughter an animal and then examine the entrails for good or bad omens.

Some old omens have turned out to have a scientific basis, and thus were not so much spiritual messages but rather simply natural occurrences.

For example: "Red sky in the morning, sailor take warning. Red sky at night, sailor's delight." This saying comes to us from English sailors, who looked westward towards the sea. If the sky in the morning looked red because the sunrise was being reflected by clouds, then a storm could be brewing. On the other hand, if the sunset was its normal red color in the evening, then the sky was clear and no stormclouds were around.

Other interesting old omens/beliefs:

* A ship's bell that rang by itself was considered an omen of death.

* Rats leaving a ship was considered bad luck.

* If the palm of your hand itches, then money is coming to you.

* If your ears feel warm or itch, then someone is talking about you.
* If a butterfly flies into your house that means a visitor is on the way.
* A cat coming into your house means bad luck.
* A dog coming into your house means good luck.
* If there is a ringing in your ears that means you will soon be receiving a message.
* If a picture or a statue of a famous person falls then something bad is about to happen to that person.
* A rabbit or a black cat crossing your path means bad luck.
* Seeing a rainbow is considered good luck. (However, we are still unsure what a double rainbow means.)

To use this method in your psychic practice, it's easy - just ask for an omen! As a matter of fact, the more you do this the better you will get at it, as you will quickly learn to decipher the messages being sent to you.

You can do this in two ways. One, simply ask for an omen regarding an upcoming an event. Simply put the request out there three times: "Send me an omen about X, send me an omen about X, send me an omen about X." Or, two, ask for a specific kind of omen, such as: "Send me an omen by the weather about X," or "Send me an omen about X by birds."

Then, when you observe something that you think might be an omen in response to your request, check your gut reaction. Ask yourself, "Was that an omen about *X*?" Then, go with your feelings.

> "It is your omen, only you know the meaning. To me, it is but another star in the night."
> ~ *Gerald R. Stanek*

> "Omens are a language, it's the alphabet we develop to speak to the world's soul, or the universe's, or God's, whatever name you want to give it. Like an alphabet, it is individual, you only learn it by making mistakes, and that keeps you from globalizing the spiritual quest."
> ~ *Paulo Coelho*

Chapter 26: Automatic Writing

Automatic writing is done by first focusing on a question while having a paper and pen in your hands, and then letting go of the question and putting your attention on something else, and just writing or doodling whatever you feel (note: *feel*, not think).

It takes a little practice to get good at it, but the insights you can get with it can be truly amazing sometimes.

To me automatic writing is a bit like surfing. It doesn't work if you're worrying about where to put your feet on the board, or whether you can catch a particular wave. You need to let go and simply *do it* without thinking about it.

Just allow the psychic guidance to flow *through* you. When we do automatic writing, we don't think about it, we just write. It's all very stream of consciousness. There's no wrong or right, and always feel free to change topics in mid-sentence or draw little doodles or whatever else feels like it needs to get expressed.

I like to write the question down, but I write it on the back of the paper that I'll be using for the automatic writing. This locks the question into my subconscious, but because it's on the back of the page I'm not tempted to look at it and *think* about it.

In general, you don't want to look at the paper while you're doing automatic writing. Your natural curiosity will want to read what you've written, and this will immediately interrupt the flow.

Sample Reading By Automatic Writing

A client (let's call him Jack) emailed me a question: Will I get a good price for my house if I put it on the market right now?

Later that evening, I watched a meditation video, which had lots of beautiful pictures and soft relaxing music.

I did an invocation for clear psychic guidance from the Light and I wrote the question on the back of a piece of paper: Will Jack get a good price for his house if he puts it on the market right now? Then I propped myself up with some pillows, with the paper and pen in my hand, and focused on the video. Here's what I got:

* A bunch of scribbles (I like to start out with some scribbles first, to make sure the pen works)
* Some "U" shapes that kind of looked like smiles
* Some boxy looking things
* The letter "A" a few times
* The number 280, written heavily
* A long spiral shape followed by the word "Yep!"
* The words "No deal," again written heavily
* More scribbly stuff

When I discussed this later with Jack, he told me that he had considered $280,000 (notice how "two eight" kind of sounds like "u" and "a"?) as his starting high price. Based on the reading, he stuck with this number, and even told his broker "no deal" when offered $275,000. And the buyer finally agreed to $280,000!

Chapter 27: Psychometry

We all leave energetic imprints on the items that we touch, particularly those things that we own or may touch often.

Psychometry is the divinatory art of obtaining psychic information about an object or its owner through contact with or proximity to the object.

For people who are kinesthetic and whose preferred sense is touch, psychometry can be much easier than trying to get visions or hear a psychic voice.

> "Psychometry is one of the easiest psychic abilities to develop."
> ~ *Ted Andrews (1952-2009), author, "How To Do Psychic Readings Through Touch"*

It is very easy to do. You just hold an object that belongs to someone else, and ask yourself a specific question regarding the object or its owner, and notice the psychic response that you get.

Some people say that it is easier to pick up information from metallic objects than non-metallic objects, but as you develop your psychometric skills you may find that it's just as easy, or even easier, for you to get psychic impressions from clothing, beloved objects such as books or personal items, and so forth.

I would make a cautionary note, though, regarding beloved old family heirlooms that may have had a series of owners, each imprinting the object with their energies, as all of these energies can make an item very complicated and confusing to read.

The psychic response can be as complicated as a series of visions and voiced guidances to something as simple as a feeling of warmth, or pressure, or lightness, or perhaps a color, or a sound. Don't try to interpret the response until you feel it has finished.

Billet readings are a popular form of psychometry practiced in some spiritualist churches.

Before the church service, people put a piece of paper into a bowl, and then during the service one of the ministers or readers will reach into the bowl and draw out one of the pieces of paper and gave a short reading for the person based upon the psychic impressions that the minister received in response to a silently-asked question, usually something like: "What is Spirit's message for this person at this time? What is coming for this person in the next week?"

In churches that I served as a minister, we would usually have a stack of small papers with a word written twice on it.

People would randomly take these pieces of paper and then rip them in half, keeping one part with the word on it and putting the other part (which also had the word on it) into the bowl.

When a minister or reader drew the paper from the bowl, he/she would announce the word before giving the reading, so that the person getting the reading would know that it was for them, while the minister or reader would not know the identity of the person getting the reading.

Sample Psychometry Reading

    A friend (we'll call her Beth) had been experiencing dreams and feelings of visitations from a favorite aunt (we'll call her Sarah), who had recently passed, and she wondered what the purpose of the visits and dreams was.

    She brought me a ring that she had given to her aunt, and which her aunt had enjoyed and worn often.

    We sat in the reading area in my home, and lit some candles and placed an amethyst crystal on the table and invoked the light of psychic and spiritual guidance.

    I held the ring in my left hand and cupped my right hand over it, and closed my eyes and let my mind relax, and I mentally repeated three times the question: "If Sarah has a message for Beth, what is the message?" †

    I immediately felt a feeling of warmth in the room, and had a vision of a smiling, kindly-looking older woman, wearing a purple shawl with a large brass-colored brooch with a green gemstone on it. I sensed a strong message of love, and the words "It's OK" or "I'm OK." This continued for a few minutes, and when I felt that there would be nothing else to the message I sent my thanks and gratitude for the message and opened my eyes.

Beth told me that she had been sad and crying since her aunt had passed, and had wondered if her aunt was in a good place with no suffering since she had passed.

When I described my vision she confirmed that her aunt had often worn such a purple shawl, with a brass-colored brooch with a green gemstone on it.

Beth also said that she had felt her aunt's presence and that the flames on the candles had visibly grown in size and gave off some sparks during the reading. (This was kind of unusual.)

We both felt that the dreams and visitations were probably caused by Beth's sadness, and that her Aunt Sarah had been wanting to send a message of comfort and love, and that things were OK for her now.

I told Beth that she needed to get over her sadness, as it was (apparently) keeping Sarah from moving on to the spiritual world in peace. I suggested that she might focus instead on her love and positive feelings for her aunt while she had been alive.

† Doing psychometry readings with items belonging to third persons usually raises ethical issues. In this case, though, the person had passed, and we phrased the question in a respectful way that didn't pry into matters beyond Beth and Sarah's relationship. Beth was with me the whole time and I merely acted as her proxy. Also, by sharing her message of love, Sarah apparently was OK with the process and consented to this kind of communication.

Chapter 28: Aura Reading

The aura is an energy field that surrounds and permeates the physical body that can be seen and felt. The colors observed in the aura may reveal facts regarding the physical body, such as mood and health.

Some people can also scry another person's aura, and see visions in the aura related to the person.

> "The vital force is not enclosed in man, but radiates round him like a luminous sphere."
> ~ *Paracelsus (1493-1541), Swiss physician*

Special note: Obtaining psychic information regarding another person, including by reading their aura, is an invasion of their privacy, and should only be done with their consent.

There are many ways to observe auras. You can see your own aura by pointing your two index fingers at each other, separated by about ½ to 1 inch, with a light or white surface in the background. Stare at the point between the fingers. You may soon start seeing a light gray area around the fingers. You may also see the auras between the two fingertips connect. Move the fingertips slightly apart to see how far the connection holds. Slightly move one finger up and down in relation to the other finger, and notice how the gray area keeps the fingertips connected.

You can also physically feel your own aura. First, rub the palms of your hands together. Then hold the palms facing each other about eight inches apart and slowly bring them together until you feel resistance. It may feel like you have a soft squishy ball between your hands. These are the auric fields pressing against each other.

Next, point one of your index fingers at (but don't touch) the palm of the other hand and slowly move it around. You should be able to feel the aura energy from your fingertip on your palm as it moves. It may feel like a tickling sensation, or like someone is blowing air lightly onto your palm.

To see another person's aura, have the person stand against a blank wall (some people see auras easier when the person is in front of a light-colored wall, and others when the person is in front of a dark-colored wall - whatever works best for you is OK). Make sure that they are not casting a shadow on the wall, as this can be distracting. Stare at a spot in the middle of their forehead.

Again, after a while, you should begin to see a thin band of gray around the person. Don't look at it directly at this stage or it will disappear. Just keep looking at the point you started with. As you keep looking, you may begin to notice that there are faint colors in the gray. For me, they appear to be sort of pastel colors. As you keep looking the colors will get stronger. At this point, you will probably be able to look at the aura directly and it shouldn't go away.

If you don't have another person to work with you may be able to view your own aura using a large mirror.

You can also feel another person's aura. Stand behind them, and rub the palms of your hands together vigorously for about 15-20 seconds. Then place your hands about 6 to 10 inches away from the sides of their head, and slowly move your hands towards their head until you feel resistance.

You won't need to touch them physically, just get close. If you aren't feeling their aura by the time your hands are only an inch or two away, try rubbing your hands together again, and also ask them to mentally focus on something spiritual. Then try again putting your hands outside the sides of their head and slowly move your hands closer to the head until you feel resistance. It may be a very light feeling, so try and be sensitive to anything that you feel on the palms of your hands.

Once you've located the aura near the head, you can slowly move your hands around the shoulders and arms, and notice the different thicknesses and feelings in their aura.

Animals and plants have auras that can be sensed or seen.

As with everything, the more you do it the better you'll get at it. So practice often!

Reading Auras

Aura readings are generally done by noticing the colors in a person's aura and then interpreting the meaning of the colors.

Common interpretations of some of the colors seen in auras include:

* Red generally indicates personal life force and vitality. It can also reflect passion and aggressiveness.

* Orange often symbolizes creativity, sometimes including fertility and sexuality.

* Yellow generally reflects mental activity or intellectual capability.

* Green is associated with love, healing, and prosperity and abundance. When green is an indicator of healing energies, it may be that the person is undergoing healing or that they have a natural talent as a healer.

* Blue may symbolize serenity and peacefulness, spiritual interests, or a talent for communication and expression.

* Dark blues, such as indigo, violet blue or imperial blue, often indicate strong spirituality and/or psychic or intuitive abilities.

* Purple is commonly associated with advanced spiritual development.

* Brown generally represents the energies of being practical, materially-oriented, and having good common sense.

*	Gray often reflects feelings of lacking focus and being scattered energetically. Gray can also sometimes indicate illness.

*	Black often indicates fear or blocking or a blockage. The person may be afraid or hiding something.

*	Sparkling silver in the aura of a woman may be a sign that she is pregnant or going to be pregnant soon.

There are also plenty of lists on the Internet regarding the meaning of many more of the colors that we may see in the aura. These meanings can be subjective, though, and so may not be correct for you.

The best way to really know what each color means is to view your own aura using a mirror and notice the colors and your own condition at the time.

So check your aura and notice the colors that you see when you are: happy, sad, depressed, confident, sick, healthy, angry, relaxed, on medication, feeling poor, feeling wealthy, and so forth. This will tell you what the colors in the aura truly mean to you.

Chapter 29: Direct Psychic Readings

Readings performed using clairvoyance (clear seeing), clairaudience (clear hearing), or any of the other "clairs" are based simply on using one's psychic skills. The reader sends out a specific question and then observes her inner visions, listens to her inner voices, or otherwise obtains the psychic response and then discusses what she saw or heard with the client.

These types of readings usually also don't need any special tools to do them, although many readers do go into a light trance in order to do the reading, and therefore it may be most suitable to conduct these kinds of readings in a quiet place where you won't be disturbed.

If you feel that you have sufficiently developed your psychic abilities to do this kind of reading, there are basically five steps to using this method. While the discussion below is somewhat extensive, in practice you will find that you can often do this kind of reading in a matter of moments once you're good at it.

The five steps are:
* Create a clear, well-formed question for the reading
* Go into a relaxed, receptive mental state
* Send out the question
* Receive the response
* Interpret and confirm the response

We've already discussed how to create a clear, well-formed question (Chapter 18), as well as how to put your mind into a relaxed, meditative state.

Be sure to eliminate any possible distractions or intrusions by taking care of any bodily needs, turning telephones and televisions off, etc. If you have just been very active, either physically or mentally, take a moment to recover so that you will be able to relax and center.

Don't play "relaxing" music or use other light or sound devices, as these may stimulate associated memories that are unrelated to the psychic/intuitive guidance you are seeking.

Just make your body comfortable and relaxed. Center yourself. Gently allow your mind to go into a quiet and relaxed meditative state.

Sending Out The Question

When you are relaxed and ready, ask the question three times slowly, focusing your intent on the question. You can ask the question silently in your mind or out loud - whichever feels right.

The important thing is that, while you are asking the question, your intent is clearly focused on the question without distraction.

Then open your awareness to be ready to receive the psychic response. While the response will commonly come through your primary psychic sense - whether that be visual imagery, sounds or words, sensations in the body, or simply a sudden knowing - be mindful that it may come to you in another of those ways as well.

Receiving The Response

Allow any images, words, sensations, or communications to come naturally to your mind. Do not try to force them, guide them, interpret them, or in any other way react to them. Simply let them come and unfold in your mind.

Avoid interpreting while receiving. When we begin receiving psychic information during a reading, our brain's first reaction will be to try to interpret the information and give it context so we can understand it. But that can interfere with the accuracy of the information being received.

This can be the "hard" part of the process - just letting the images, sounds, and so forth come into your mind without trying to immediately interpret or otherwise "understand" them. The conscious mind will automatically want to jump in and start "making sense" of what you are experiencing. Unfortunately, this usually means that the conscious mind will then lead you into directions that it is already familiar with, which may be very different from the psychic message. So just let the images, words, or feelings come without any interpreting.

After the psychic impressions have stopped coming (usually no more than a few minutes), come back into a full waking state, and write down or otherwise record as much as you can remember of the images, feelings, words, sounds, etc. that you experienced.

Instead of waiting to return from the psychic state, some people record their impressions while in the psychic state by describing the impressions that they get while they are getting them by speaking into a tape recorder or writing on a pad of paper without looking at the pad. Again, just do what feels most comfortable and natural for you. There is no "right" way - just your way.

But do record the impressions in one way or another as soon as possible after receiving them to ensure the best accuracy. If you trust your memory, you may well find that the conscious mind will continue to try to "make sense" of the impressions, and may devise a "meaning" for the actual information that you received.

Interpreting The Response

Now that we have received and recorded the psychic images, words, sounds, sensations and other impressions, we may discover their meaning by interpreting them.

Studies have revealed that, for over 90% of us, the left hemispheres of our brains are the language-dominant hemispheres.

This leaves the intuition-connected right hemispheres to communicate in something other than language. As a result, much psychic information that we receive is symbolic. Mastering the hidden language of your own mind can be a powerful key to true self-knowledge and empowerment.

Although you sometimes may receive messages that are quite clear immediately (for example, a voice saying "Buy XYZ stock now!"), the right brain generally communicates symbolically, in a "language" that can be very unique and different from the "language" that another person's brain may use. It will be up to you to learn to understand the specific symbolism that your own psychic mind uses, as we discussed in Chapter 6.

Of course, you should discuss in detail with the seeker, whether a friend or a client, the images, sounds, and so forth, that you received, as that information might make more sense to them than it does to you.

If no interpretation of the results leads you to an answer, then - assuming that you have indeed used a well-formed question - you may consider refining the question a bit and trying again to get additional clues. For example, if your first question was "will I be happier with X or Y?", try the method again just using "will I be happy with X?" and then "will I be happy with Y?" and compare the results to see if you're getting a better sense of direction.

If you still can't get a clear answer, then you might first take a break, and clear your head by taking a walk, having a meal, or otherwise busying yourself with some mundane activity for a bit.

Then when you return to your psychic explorations, try asking a question about the initial question, such as: "Can I get a clear answer to the question '(whatever your question was)' now?" Or try consulting with your psychic guides (see the next chapter) to see if they can shed some light on why you could not get a clear answer to the question at this time.

The sooner that you can determine the difference between a message from your psychic guidance and, for example, an emotion triggered by an association with an old memory, then the sooner that you will be able to really benefit from psychic insights and the less likely that you will be misled by misinterpretations.

Determining True Psychic Responses From Imagination

Here is one good way to tell the differences between real psychic information and non-psychic information, or imagination:

Whenever you have an accurate psychic insight, such as when the phone rings and you know who's calling or you have a dream about something that comes true or something like that, as soon as possible - while the memory of the insight is still fresh in your mind - consider:

* How did you receive the information? Was it a picture in your mind? A "voice"? A sensory feeling in your body?

* What were the qualities of the message? For example, if it was a vision (still picture or movie): How big was it? Was it in color? Was it clear or somewhat fuzzy? Was it close or far away? Did it have a border, and, if so, what color (if any)? What position was it in - straight ahead of you, off to the side, up, down, or otherwise?

If a "voice" or other sound: What were the qualities of the voice/sound, the loudness, tonality, clarity, and so forth?

If a sensory feeling: Where was it located in your body? What kind of feeling was it? Again, what kinds of qualities did it have?

Once you have determined the qualities of accurate psychic insights that you receive, then compare them with the qualities of non-psychic impressions that you receive that same way.

For example, perhaps the pictures that you see in your head when you are remembering something don't have a border, but the accurate psychic insights do have one. Or the psychically-accurate "voice" that you hear has a different tone to it from the "voice" that does your normal thinking.

Note any quality differences carefully, and then watch carefully to see if those differences continue to occur in connection with accurate psychic insights that you get. The quicker you can make these kinds of determinations the quicker and stronger your psychic ability will become.

Another way to tell between true psychic guidance and our imaginations is to examine just exactly what are our own thoughts, prejudices, hopes or fears regarding the situation, and then compare those with the information that we "received." This can quickly reveal our own dispositions, and whether they are interfering with the psychic process.

Sometimes, when we directly ask for psychic guidance, the response is not as clear as we had hoped. This may occur because our initial question was not clear enough, but it can also happen sometimes because there were many possible outcomes to the situation in question, and the psychic mind was unsure as to which response was actually appropriate to the question.

One method of clarifying a response is consulting with the Higher Self or our other guides because you can ask directly: "Was that the real answer, or did I imagine that answer because it was what I wanted to hear?" Consultations with the Higher Self or guides/counselors can quite often be as prolonged as you need to get the information you seek. See the next chapter for more on this.

If the response is that the answer received came from your imagination, you can even ask the Higher Self or guides/counselors for a better way to ask the question to get an accurate result.

Another method for confirmation is using a pendulum.

Simply designate one direction of swing of the pendulum as being "x" (where "x" equals one of the possible answers) and a different swing of the pendulum as being "y" (where "y" equals the other possible answer). Then relax and let the pendulum show you the answer that your psychic guidance truly intended.

Chapter 30: Consulting Higher Self, Spirit Guides and Angels

One of the most powerful ways to obtain psychic guidance is by establishing a good relationship with your higher self and/or guides and angels.

Simply go into a relaxed state of mind and meet with them mentally and discuss the situation. You can usually ask any question that you like to get more information. These guides have the higher information that you seek. They can also explain details of situations that other techniques can only hint at.

The way to establish a relationship with your higher self (soul or spirit), spirit guides, angels, or other guides, is through an intentional meditation.

As always, be sure to eliminate any possible distractions or intrusions by taking care of any bodily needs, turning telephones and televisions off, etc. If you have just been very active, either physically or mentally, take a moment to recover so that you will be able to relax and center.

Don't play "relaxing" music or use other light or sound devices, as these may stimulate associated memories that are unrelated to the psychic/intuitive guidance you are seeking.

Just make yourself comfortable. Center yourself. Relax your body and allow your mind to go into the relaxed psychic state.

Then, in your mind, go to a "sacred place," somewhere that is very special and powerful to you, a place where you feel totally confident, peaceful and strong, and you can feel comfortable being in touch with very special spiritual energies, such as your higher self, angels, or other special guides. It might be a place that you have actually been to physically, or a place that you are attracted to spiritually, or a place that you have imagined or just heard about.

Take just a moment there to reflect on the wonderful characteristics of this place and the way it makes you feel to be there. Notice how it looks, how it feels, and just enjoy the sensation of being in that very special and sacred place.

Then think of an energy that is especially important to you, whether it's your higher self, an angel, an animal or other guide, and consider this energy as your special guide. And mentally think the words, "I invite my special guide to join me here."

Your special guide may appear as a being of light, or in a number of different forms, or you may simply become aware that a presence has joined you.

When you are aware of the presence of your special guide, then express your thanks, gratitude and love and take a moment just to observe the details of the experience, and how it feels.

And you may sense that your special guide has infinite wisdom to share, as it radiates that wisdom with dignity, joy and power.

Your special guide will always be there to guide and advise you, loving you in full acceptance and understanding of you just as you really are. In the presence of your special guide you may even sometimes notice that you just automatically receive wisdom and insights about situations and questions that you haven't even asked.

Whenever you want to meet with your special guide you can always go to your sacred place and use this method of inviting your special guide to join you there. When you are done with this meeting, express your thanks, gratitude and love. Embrace your special guide, and allow it to leave your sacred place.

Spiritual forces, like your higher self, soul or spirit, your spiritual guides and angels, loved ones who have passed on, and other spiritual forces are always around you and have your best wishes and your highest good at heart at all times. These spiritual forces are always near you and available to you whenever you need.

And you can always feel free to take a moment to ask these spiritual forces, however you might imagine them to be, the question or questions that are nearest and deepest to your heart at that time. Just pose the questions, and then let them go.

And then notice the responses that you may have gotten. It may be clear images in your mind, or just a sense of knowing, or a feeling in your body. But there is a part of you that will know what the responses were. All you need to do is quiet your mind, and listen to that part of you.

And always be sure to send gratitude and love to your spiritual forces, your guides, angels and loved ones, for how much they care and watch out for you. Because they are always there for you, whenever you need them.

> ". . . the higher self is like the seeing eye of the soul. The higher self is the soul's awareness of itself, that the soul is our true identity. ... The higher self knows the whole person - body, mind and spirit - not simply what the ego thinks of itself. Though the ego has use of the conscious mind, the higher self has access to the subconscious and the superconscious mind."
> *~ Henry Reed, Ph.D., author, "Edgar Cayce on Channeling Your Higher Self"*

Section III

Doing Psychic Readings Professionally

Chapter 31: Business Basics For Psychics

After developing their psychic abilities, and mastering a couple of psychic reading methods, some people decide to "follow their passion" and begin using their psychic skills professionally.

There are many considerations involved in starting any business, and psychic businesses are no different. In some ways they can be even more complex than traditional businesses due to stringent local laws.

In the following chapters, we'll review some successful psychic business models, common business activities that many psychics include in their practices, potential locations where personal readings may be conducted, how to create a powerful personal brand, and how to promote and market a psychic practice.

In this chapter, we'll consider some business basics and how they might apply to a professional psychic practice.

Disclaimer: I am not a lawyer, accountant, or financial planner, and nothing herein is intended to constitute legal or professional financial advice. Furthermore, given the wide variety of potentially applicable laws and regulations, this book cannot possibly begin to provide definitive guidance on those topics. Simply be aware that these may be some of the "hoops" that you may have to jump through, and please seek appropriate professional guidance whenever it might be useful or needed.

Licenses and Laws

In order to conduct any kind of business, it is usually necessary to obtain the appropriate business licenses and comply with all applicable laws, whether on the city, county, state or federal level.

The same is true for the psychic reading business, but it should be noted that many cities have special license requirements or other laws regarding psychic readings, or, as such codes commonly refer to it - "fortune-telling." Always check the municipal code and inquire with the city clerk for any city where you are considering doing business.

Some cities even have more than one kind of regulation that must be considered; for example, a city may have a special law in one part of their municipal code regarding doing readings, and another special law in a different part regarding the physical places where readings may be conducted. In a situation like that, you would need to be sure that not only your activities complied with the code but that the place where you were doing readings complied as well.

In many states, psychic-related businesses are only regulated at the municipal level, and there are no county or state laws that apply. So while one psychic, operating under a strict city code, may have to comply with a large set of regulations, another psychic just down the road but on a piece of county land where there are no applicable county laws may not have to deal with any special regulations at all.

Some cities also make exemptions for "fortune-telling" activities that are conducted by ministers of recognized churches, so such a minister may be able to conduct their activities freely. Again, though, you should always obtain competent legal guidance before proceeding on the assumption that you are exempt because of any ordinations you may hold.

The bottom line is choose carefully where you are going to conduct business, and comply with all applicable licensing requirements and laws.

Taxes and Bookkeeping

No matter where you conduct your business activities, you know that all of the applicable governing agencies are going to want their cut in the form of taxes (besides any licensing fees), so you will need to track your income and expenses and pay all taxes when due. This is true for any business. Consult a tax expert to be sure you can comply with all of the requirements.

Insurance

Almost all businesses need to carry some kind of insurance. If you are operating a physical business location, you will probably need some kind of "slip and fall" liability insurance.

But as readings may also be considered a kind of counseling, you may need some additional insurance to protect you in case you may have some liabilities in that area as well.

An insurance professional may be best able to provide competent guidance on these topics, and I encourage you to consult one if and when it may be appropriate.

Leases and Property Purchases

While many beginning psychics have dreams of setting up their own shop, which might entail leasing or buying a piece of property where this business would be conducted, in fact this should be among the last of your considerations.

Let your business do the deciding for you here. Wait until your business is so active and large that it only makes economic sense for you to obtain your own business location. As we'll see in Chapter 34, there may be many other places where you can ply your trade for little or no cost, so it doesn't make much sense to take on a regular rent or mortgage payment until your level of business literally demands it.

This is particularly true with regard to entering into a commercial lease. Commercial leases can be life-devastating landmine fields for the inexperienced. I strongly recommend that no one ever enter into a commercial lease without the guidance of an attorney well-experienced in that area.

It is far too common for many service providers, such as psychics, but also including counselors, therapists, life coaches, etc., to go out and sign a commercial office space lease and put thousands of dollars into rent, furnishings, decorations, equipment and so forth, without having the incoming business necessary to support their practice or reimburse them for their investments.

It is much more prudent economically to do your readings any place else that you can, such as at fairs, a metaphysical bookstore, a coffee shop, a public park, and so forth, until the volume of your business is so large and your income sufficient that it really becomes a necessity for you to have your own professional office.

Chapter 32: Setting Fees And Getting Paid

This is the good part! You're providing valuable services, so you are entitled to be appropriately compensated for those services. Issues for consideration include how much to charge for your services, how to process the payments, and when to get paid.

To find out how much to charge, you might call around to other local psychic businesses, or check on the Internet, to find out what other psychics may be charging for their services.

If you work at psychic fairs or metaphysical bookstores, you may find that some fairs and stores will set the rates for readers, and you can either accept the rate that they set or not work at those places. Other places may allow you to set your own rate.

There are two common business models for fairs and stores that have psychic readers.

In one model, the fair or store handles the advertising, they set the rates for readings, they process the payments received from the clients, and they pay the psychic readers a percentage of what they charge the clients.

In the other model, the fair or store simply rents space to psychic readers, and the readers are responsible for bringing in their own clients and processing their own payments.

Psychic readers who are just beginning their careers may be more attracted to the first model, because they don't have an established clientele, they don't have a method for processing credit card payments, and/or they don't have a professional space available where they can do their readings.

If you eventually establish your own independent practice, you may wish to obtain the ability to process credit card payments. Many people decide to get a reading on impulse, and may not have enough cash in their pockets at that time. If you are able to process credit payments, you can still handle those clients. I have found several services that can process credit card payments through the Internet. Of course, do your research and be sure that you're dealing with a company you can trust, but my own experience has been that there are indeed good businesses you can work with.

As to when to get paid, if you are getting paid by a fair or store then you will have to agree to get paid on the schedule that they provide. I also recommend that you (discreetly) check with other psychics who are working or have worked at that venue to find out if they always get paid the full amount that they've earned in a timely manner. Most fair producers and store owners are honest and will treat you fairly, but other possibilities exist and it's always best to avoid unpleasant surprises.

If you are working independently, I always recommend that you get paid up-front, particularly with phone reading clients. It's just easier to get the money issues out of the way first, so that you can focus on doing a good reading and not need to worry.

Chapter 33: Psychic Business Models And Activities

I've observed several basic business models that people generally use to develop a professional psychic practice. The first two models make most of their income from readings, while the rest usually make most of their income from other sources and may do readings as an adjunct to their primary business.

These business models are:
* The Personal Reader
* The Phone Reader
* The Teacher
* The Author
* The Consultant
* The Professional Speaker
* The Stage Performer
* The Spiritual Leader

Each of these models may use a variety of methods for generating income from their activities.

The Personal Reader: Personal readers generally build and maintain steady client bases for private readings, as well as perhaps doing local fairs and parties. A typical reader's life commonly includes doing personal and phone readings, writing, promotional efforts, and personal development.

Beginning readers might consider working as a reader at psychic fairs, "alternative lifestyle" events, metaphysical stores, private home parties, and any other opportunity to practice their trade, gain experience, and build their clientele.

Home psychic parties work something like Tupperware and other home "parties." The "hostess" agrees to use her home to host a group of her friends who are interested in meeting with a professional psychic. The psychic normally puts on a small demonstration or talk for the group, and then retires to a private room and the guests come in one at a time to get short private readings.

Sometimes the guests pay the psychic individually, and sometimes the hostess arranges to pay the psychic for the event as a gift to her guests or else she makes her own arrangements for repayment from her guests. The hostess usually also gets a free reading, a special crystal, or some other compensation from the psychic for arranging the party.

Readers may also find opportunities to work at larger parties scheduled around certain holidays, like Halloween. While these kinds of parties can be quite lucrative, they can also be long and exhausting, so make sure that you are provided time for breaks and either bring a lunch or otherwise have some access to food and beverages to keep your strength up.

The Phone Reader: Phone readers enjoy the convenience of working from home or are not drawn to doing in-person readings or fairs. Because their clients come from a wider base (often from Internet or print advertising), however, they usually don't get the benefit of the word-of-mouth promotion that personal readers do. So it can be important for them to get client testimonials that they can post to their websites or the services that they work through.

Many phone readers work for companies that run massive amounts of advertising and charge high per-minute fees, while only paying the psychics a small percentage of that.

Some of the popular websites that psychics can do telephone readings through include keen.com and kooma.com. I have not done business with either of these companies, so I can't speak from any personal experience. If you are exploring the option of working with these companies I simply encourage you to do your own investigations and choose your associations wisely.

It is certainly possible, though, to simply advertise and sell your own phone readings without going through a company, but then you'll need to have a method to process the client's payment, since you won't be seeing them in person to receive cash. For my own phone readings, I accept credit card payments over the Internet, or else I allow people to pay in advance by mailing me a check or money order.

Besides the telephone, some psychics also do readings by email, direct mail, texting, or other remote communication method.

Some readers are now using Skype and similar Internet video services to be able to provide remote face-to-face readings by webcam.

The Teacher: Teachers earn money from providing classes, workshops and seminars, although they may also get income from producing books, websites, and other instructional media. Many teachers, including me, started out as readers, and then began teaching in response to interest that they got from their clients.

Opportunities for teaching classes, seminars, workshops, and so forth can be found in many places, from schools and universities to someone's home, bookstores, metaphysical stores and centers, and community centers.

The requirements for producing classes vary by the location. For example, hosting a small psychic development class in your own home that you advertise though flyers distributed locally can be a very fast and easy way to start generating some side income. At the other end of the scale, doing a multi-day seminar at a large hotel may entail many months of preparation and promotion, and paying some hefty expenses up-front.

The Author: The author business model is simply to publish original content, and it is from their books, articles, etc., that authors make most of their income. They may also generate additional money from doing readings, workshops, seminars, etc.

If you enjoy writing, then this may be a good path for you. It can be a little tricky to get started, as most publishing houses these days prefer not to do business directly with writers, but rather insist that they be represented by an agent, but for those who are truly ambitious and dedicated it is certainly doable.

Many authors get their start by writing a blog or doing articles or regular columns for small publications or websites. Daily astrology or card readings, advice columns, stories, "how-to" articles, and so forth can be a good way to get started and build up a fan base.

Some authors also create and sell Tarot card sets, psychic reading games or devices, CDs or DVDs.

Many new authors, who haven't yet acquired the fame of a Doreen Virtue or a Sylvia Browne, end up doing self-publishing, some with the hope of having a professional publishing house picking up their book for a regular publishing in the future.

Amazon, Smashwords, BookBaby, Barnes & Noble, Lulu and Booktango all currently offer options for self-publishing. The field is complex, however, so new authors should do plenty of investigation and study before choosing their publishing route.

The Consultant: Some psychics specialize in working with businesses, such as by providing private business consulting or training staff on how to increase their intuitive awareness.

In this area it's usually good to maintain a very professional appearance and to promote your services using top-quality marketing materials. The route to success is commonly to start out consulting with small businesses for low fees, get good testimonials from them, and then market your way up the ladder.

The Professional Speaker: Professional speakers usually are very knowledgeable on specific metaphysical topics, and must be able to talk to groups of 10 to a thousand people or more. They can make much of their money from their speaking fees, but sometimes make even more from the sales of books, CDs, etc., at their speaking events, or may charge high rates for private readings. Some professional speakers travel a lot, and spend much of their time a long way from their homes. On the plus side, though, famous and sought-after professional speakers can make a great deal of money for their efforts.

Finding work as a public speaker can be somewhat slow at the start unless the psychic has first created a degree of fame or celebrity by writing popular books or regularly appearing in the news or other media.

The Stage Performer: The life of a stage performer may be very similar to that of the professional speaker. However, rather than focusing on speaking, the stage performer's presentations are usually limited to giving readings or demonstrations to their audiences. While some people may find it hard to relax enough in order to give good readings in front of a large audience, those that are able to do so may be able to find both fame and fortune.

The Spiritual Leader: Spiritual leaders devote most of their efforts to building and maintaining a spiritually-centered community, such as a New Thought, New Age, metaphysical or spiritualist church, and derive their income from those activities, while perhaps providing readings or psychic counseling as a way of generating additional income.

This path is a relatively rare calling, and can be quite long and difficult with many challenges along the way, but for those who are drawn to it there can be much satisfaction and fulfillment.

Quite often, people new to this path may need to:

* Advertise the church or organization, give public talks, network with spiritual seekers, and otherwise act to locate a core group of people who can form the base of the community or congregation

* Secure a location for meetings or services to be held

* Lead those meetings or services

* Keep advertising, seek referrals, write and print newsletters and articles, etc. to keep the community or congregation growing

* As the community/congregation grows, start selecting and grooming leaders from the group to help assume management and development of the group

It's often a full-time process, and requires loving care and devotion. In the beginning stages, there is usually no money for salaries, as any donations/income must be put right back into continuing to grow the community/congregation. As a rule of thumb, the community/congregation usually needs to number at least 200 people before sufficient donations are being received to allow the leader to start to drawing a salary.

Of course, in a field with so many unique opportunities, there are plenty of folks who combine two or more of the models described above to create their own individual model that best suits themselves. In my own career, I have done, or am doing, all of the above except stage performing.

Should you find yourself feeling drawn towards more than one model, please do not let these descriptions limit you, and feel free to create your own business model that best expresses the uniqueness of you!

Chapter 34: Locations For Doing Readings

If you are thinking about setting up a private professional office for your readings, and you have access to any other possible place to do readings, then you should most likely not get a private office yet. Having your own private professional office in a commercial building is probably the most expensive way to go, and so it should not be the way to start.

Instead, allow your business to create the demand and pay for the office. Creative thinking may reveal many low or no cost places near you where you can do readings in the meanwhile.

Your Home or the Client's Home

Doing the reading at your home or the client's home is often the easiest and least expensive option. It's usually quiet and private, with comfortable seating and other amenities. I have done lots of readings at my clients' homes, and this may be an option for you. I understand, though, that many female readers are not at ease with the idea of strangers coming into their personal residence. This is an issue you will have to resolve for yourself.

Public Parks

When I was first starting out, I often would do readings in public parks or gardens. As a matter of fact, if it's a particularly pretty park or garden or there's a good view, the setting can be nicer and more inspirational than most offices!

The problems that may arise with using public parks or gardens are generally, 1) the weather, 2) distractions from other visitors to the park or garden, 3) local laws prohibiting doing readings there, and 4) distractions from bugs, insects, and other local creatures.

Still, if you explore the local parks and gardens, and you've made sure you're OK with the law, you may be able to find certain spots that are quiet and secluded enough to suit your purposes.

I was even able to locate two nice areas in local parks where there were somewhat secluded pools of water that I could use for readings by scrying. I would bring some crystals and meet my clients at the park and do the reading by gazing into the pool or the crystals. And all that passers-by would see was two people sitting next to a pool of water with some crystals and chatting.

As far as cost goes, many public parks may charge a parking or entry fee. Again, check this sort of stuff out in advance and clearly inform your client, to avoid any unpleasant surprises.

Bars and Coffee Shops

Untold thousands of readings have been performed in bars, coffee shops, nightclubs, cafes, restaurants, and similar places where people may congregate for food, drink and socializing.

These types of readings generally fall into two categories: one, where the psychic performs readings for money for the existing clientele at the establishment, and the other, where the psychic brings his or her clientele to the establishment for the readings.

The first category is usually conducted in the manner of street readings, also sometimes referred to as "busking." The psychic goes into a busy establishment and performs a free reading or two, and soon has a group of people gathering around eager and willing to pay for readings for themselves.

In situations where the management is not receptive to someone coming in and "working" their clientele, this opportunity may be short-lived and the psychic may soon be shown the door. In order for a psychic to be able to do this dependably, it is usually wiser to get management's permission first or, at least, make sure that the bartender or manager is well-tipped.

The other approach is to find an establishment that is quiet during certain hours and then invite your clients to meet you there during those quiet times. This can be beneficial for both the psychic and the establishment, as it brings more business for the establishment while giving the psychic a comfortable place to do readings at little or no expense.

In fact, you may find that some bars and coffee shops will even allow you to openly advertise that you are providing readings at their establishment, to encourage more people to come. Again, though, your best bet is to always discuss your plans with the manager first, to get their permission and also their own input on how both you and the establishment may best benefit.

I have often used a coffee shop near my home for readings. There are some tables in a quiet area of the shop off to the side, and the staff has always been accepting of my occasional visits as long as we bought an occasional coffee or other refreshment.

Potential problem areas may 1) distractions from other people at the establishment, and 2) local laws prohibiting doing readings there. Hopefully, if there are no legal issues, you've got a good relationship with the establishment management and they will back you up with regard to any issues that may arise from other customers there.

Metaphysical Stores and Psychic Fairs

Psychics commonly flock to metaphysical bookstores and fairs for a moderate-cost setting in which to do readings. The big advantage is that these places are commonly visited by the kind of people who buy psychic readings, and are part of the local metaphysically-interested community, which can lead to the psychic picking up quite a bit of business and building their reputation within the community.

Metaphysical bookstores and fairs are also usually geared towards being a "reading-friendly" environment as well, and are often decorated and maintained appropriately.

As discussed before, another big plus for psychics just starting out is that established metaphysical businesses quite commonly are equipped to process credit cards, while the practitioner meeting clients at parks and coffee shops must usually only take cash or checks. Having credit card processing available can open your practice up to a greater number of potential clients, and especially "impulse buyers" who decide to get a reading on a whim but aren't carrying enough cash with them.

The downside to using bookstores and fairs, of course, is the increased cost over the types of venues previously discussed. Many bookstores and fairs will take a percentage of the psychic's income, commonly ranging from 20% to 50% and up.

Nevertheless, many beginning psychic readers choose to start their careers by taking advantage of these types of venues. The support of the community, easy access to new clients, a reading-friendly environment, and other amenities such as credit card processing seem to be more than enough compensation for the percentages paid out.

Shared Offices and Executive Suites

Even if a psychic feels compelled to use a professional private space, it's quite commonly not necessary to sign a lengthy commercial lease right at the start.

There are already thousands of psychics, energy healers, Reiki and Feng Shui practitioners, hypnotherapists, and other similar "alternative" service providers who may be happy to share their own business offices or premises with a psychic reader in exchange for a percentage of the psychic's income or a flat fee.

In fact, if there is a good-sized metaphysical business community in your area, you may even hear of people looking for others to share the use, and expense, of their business premises.

These opportunities can range from the great to the horrible, however, and should always be approached with both eyes wide open.

Good questions to have in mind when considering an offer to share space might include:

* How easy will it be for me to have access to the space? Will I have my own key?

* How often can I have access to the space?

* What are the possible resolutions if we both want to use the space at the same time?

* What does it cost for me to use the space?

*　　If the other person has a lease or rental agreement, are they allowed to sub-lease to you?

　　*　　What liabilities might you incur if the other person stops paying rent or skips town? Will the landlord try to hold you responsible for the entire lease?

Executive suites can also provide an alternative to renting a full-time location. For a regular monthly fee, professional buildings offering "executive suites" generally may provide limited access to a small generic office or conference room, mail services, and telephone and/or receptionist services.

So, for example, let's say that you charge $100 an hour for private readings, and you've been doing the readings at a local metaphysical bookstore with reading rooms and they're taking 50% of your fee. They are essentially charging you $50 per hour for the use of their reading room.

But let's say that there was also an executive suite building nearby that would give you 16 hours of access to a private office for $160 per month. If you could get 16 hours of readings per month, you'd only be spending $10 per hour for the room, which is a sizable reduction over that bookstore rate. Even if you were only getting four readings per month, you'd still be saving money over the 50% bookstore rate, as you would be paying $40 per hour for the room at the executive suite (160 divided by 4 equals 40) rather than the $50 per hour for the room at the bookstore.

You should note, though, that most executive suites only offer their services during regular business hours (approximately 9:00 am to 6:00 pm) during the weekdays. If you want more access than that, be sure to include this in your discussions before signing any agreements.

Chapter 35: Creating A Powerful Personal Brand

Now that we've had an opportunity to review the basic methods and ways that professional psychics can make money, we need to start putting all the parts together to create your professional brand and image. Your "brand" is going to be a key element in your work to advertise and market your business.

Providing professional psychic readings and so forth is a service industry, in which the psychic herself is the "product." You and your skills are what the client is buying. As a professional psychic, then, you want to "package" yourself in a way that will be attractive to clients and make them want to purchase your services.

Your preferred business activities and reading methods must be taken into consideration here, so that you may make a natural, coherent and congruent presentation of yourself in pursuit of your profession.

Following are some questions that should help you clarify your professional brand and image. Take your time - this is not a section that you should rush through, and you should feel free to use additional paper, or even notebooks, to include everything you think is important. And you may find that your answers to the questions become more refined as time goes by and your practice and goals become more clearly defined. It's not a task for an hour or two, but more like a work-in-progress for a lifetime. Yours!

What Are Your Goals?

As Alice in Wonderland reminded us earlier, it's hard to know which way to go if you don't know where you want to get to.

Goals should be simply and concisely stated, in a positive manner, and with a deadline attached. Goals are not wants or desires. They are things we plan to accomplish.

This book is an example of a tool for accomplishing a goal. It was written for people who wish to do psychic readings, and it walks you through each of the steps necessary to accomplish that goal, from developing psychic abilities to learning reading methods to marketing reading services.

Now we're coming to the point where you need to grow beyond the book and start making your own mark in the world. So, decide on your goals, write them down, and review them daily, to remind yourself and help keep yourself on the road to success.

Examples might be: "I will be a full-time Tarot reader with over 100 active clients by (month/year)." "I will write two books per year, and my first/next book will be (title) and will be published by (month/year)." "I will be a popular stage performing psychic with at least one booking per month by (month/year)."

_____

_____

_____

_____

Who Are Your Role Models?

Having strong role models in mind can help you clarify what you want to accomplish and make other decisions regarding your professional image.

Consider everyone you know who is succeeding in your chosen career path. What makes them attractive to you? How did they get to where they are? What steps do you need to take to get to the same place? How do they establish their own brand and image? How will your professional life reflect those models?

_____

_____

_____

_____

What Tools Will You Need? Where And How Will You Get Them?

The tools and spaces necessary to do readings using cards or crystals are very different from those needed by professional speakers. Determining these basics is usually the first step. Do you need a table with two chairs? An auditorium with a podium? A quiet space with a computer to write books and articles?

_____

_____

_____

_____

What/Who Is Your Target Market?

Are you going to be presenting private readings to individuals, workshops for community groups, or seminars for corporations? What professional image is best suited to that market and the business activities you will be doing? These various people will have different expectations and will make judgments about you, your credibility, your skills, and so forth, based upon how you present yourself. Take a moment to write down your target market and the image you want to project to be attractive to them.

_____

_____

_____

_____

What Resources Do You Have? Who Is On Your Team?

Making sure that you have the resources and support you need is important for every step you take on your career path. There may be many things that can help you along the way. Take the time to get those things set up first, so that when you start your career you know there are nets below that might help save you in case you make a misstep.

What resources are available to you in developing your career? Who might be good members of your support team?

Examples of personal resources and support team members might include:

- Your own genuine real passion for your work, which can give you the motivation necessary to overcome obstacles along the way

- Strong practical experience with your professional skills

- All the "tools of the trade" you might need

- Familiarity with business basics and applicable laws

- A clear business plan, including an honest assessment of what might go wrong and what "Plan B's" you might be able to plug in should that happen

- Financial support in case your earnings aren't as high as expected

- Friendships with people who have taken the same career path and can help mentor or advise you

- Supportive and non-judgmental personal relationships with people who are close to you

Take a moment to note the resources and team members you have already, as well as the ones that you still need to develop.

_____
_____
_____
_____
_____

What's The Theme Of Your Marketing Materials?

You may not ready just yet to make final decisions on this - and you may even decide to eventually consult with a professional designer at some time - but just start giving some thought to themes or other coordinated features that you will want to include in your marketing materials (business cards, flyers, websites, etc.), to maintain that sense of congruency and coherency in your presentations, and make a few notes on that now.

_____

_____

_____

_____

What Is Your "Personal Signature"?

A "personal signature" relates to a continuing theme in your marketing materials, your readings/teachings, your dress, etc. It could be anything - feathers, a yin-yang symbol, the color aqua, a cross, a particular item or kind of clothing, whatever. It's just something that helps distinguish you from others, and creates one specific thing that ties everything that you do together.

_____

_____

_____

_____

What Makes You "Special?"

A great secret truth in the psychic industry is that people love to get readings or instructed by people who are somehow "special." They do not particularly want to get readings from Andy AverageGuy. To improve your chance of being a real success in this field, you should find some way to show that you are somehow "larger than life."

Do you come from a long family line of psychics and healers? Did your abilities suddenly come upon you during a raging electrical storm? Were you instructed by some famous teacher? Do you teach secrets that you learned during a near-death experience? Was your grandmother a witch? Did you have a psychic experience when you were very young? Have you ever predicted a famous event? Did you have a transformational dream? Have you had out-of-body experiences?

There are hundreds of ways that we might be considered "special," and that includes you! Dig deep in your memory, and your family history, and try to discover them all. The more the better! What makes you special?

_____
_____
_____
_____
_____

Chapter 36: Marketing Your Professional Psychic Practice

OK, so you've developed your psychic abilities, you've mastered your chosen reading methods, you know where and how you're going to ply your trade, your professional image, your goals, your professional ethics, and you're ready to get to work. Now all you need is clients!

Most professional psychics are not good at marketing. They may be wonderful at their craft, but they don't understand how to advertise their services. This is the area that many psychics pay the least attention to - but should be paying the most attention to!

After all, you could be the best psychic in the world, but if nobody knows about you, what does it matter? Your particular chosen craft may be the heart of your business, but marketing and promotion is its life's blood.

In the following pages, we'll review more good marketing techniques than most professional psychics have even heard of, much less implemented. The benefit for you is that, by putting these techniques to work, you can have a more advanced career within a year than many people have achieved in twenty years.

Word of Mouth

Almost all professional psychics will agree that "word of mouth" advertising is the best, and it is really necessary for the top levels of success in this field. When people want to find a good psychic, they often turn to their friends for recommendations. So - lock this into your brain now - people who get readings from you need to be referring their friends to you.

If you're good, and people like getting readings from you or reading your books or taking your classes, this will happen to some degree on its own. People will occasionally refer their friends, and slowly your business will grow.

And that's how it is for most psychics. They do their best to be good psychics, and people do recommend them to their friends, but it's a slow process and leaves the psychic at the mercy of what they hope is good word-of-mouth going on out there.

That's not the best way to go. To be a success in this business, <u>you need to take control of this process</u> and develop and implement a program to actively encourage people to recommend your services.

Referrals are also the best and cheapest advertising you can get, and referred people are the least likely to want to "shop around" or feel "buyer's remorse." And yet, very, very few professional psychics have formal referral systems in place.

The key is: <u>if you want referrals, you need to ask for them.</u>

You need to create and implement a formal referral system. In fact, for the greatest success, you'll want to have many such systems in place.

For example, you'll want clients to refer you, of course, but you also want your former teachers to refer you, you want students of your classes to refer you, you want bookstores to refer you, you want authors to refer you in their books and articles, and so on.

Reach out to all of these groups and get them on your team!

So let's consider some ways to structure formal referral systems. As an example, let's apply this to getting more reading clients, as these are usually the most common and the most important part of the system for professional psychic readers.

Let's say that Jane has a reading with you, and at the end of the reading she's really happy and raving about how good you are. This is precisely the moment to take advantage and get Jane into your referral system.

So you say to Jane: "Jane, I'm very glad that you were happy with your reading. First, do you mind if I quote you on my website and other testimonials as long as I just use your first name or initials? Also, you know I'm trying to grow my business, and the best way for that to happen is for people to refer me to their friends. Here are some of my cards. If you would pass these on to your friends that could also use a reading I would really appreciate it, and it would help make sure that I could stay in this business and be there for you the next time you call."

OK, so that creates a little psychological pressure. And maybe Jane will hand out the cards and encourage her friends to visit you. But we can do better. Here's an idea that you might try instead. Say to Jane:

"Jane, you know I'm trying to grow my business, and the best way for that to happen is for people to refer me to their friends. Here are some of my cards. And here's what I'm going to do. I'm going to put a little 'J' on the back of the cards here. And for every one of these cards that comes back to me and the person gets a reading I'm going to give you 15 minutes credit towards a free reading. So if two of these cards come back you get a free half hour, if 3 come back you get 45 minutes free, and so forth."

OK, now we're talking Jane's language! She loved your reading, and you just gave her a way to get another reading free! So, is she going to hand out your cards and encourage her friends to come see you? You bet!

And what is the cost to you? Really nothing, except a little of your time. No cash outlay except the cost of the few business cards that you gave her.

Now you need to do the same thing with your former teachers, students of your classes, local metaphysical bookstores, people who are writing books and articles, and so forth.

Approach each one with the proposition of what can I do for you that will make it worthwhile for you to refer me? Create a formal referral system with each and every one of them.

Quite often, that system will just be a cross-referral. Maybe you refer people looking for classes to your former teacher, and she refers people looking for readings to you. Maybe you refer a particular author's books, and she includes a story or two about you in her next publication.

You can see this kind of cross-referral thing in the testimonials in celebrities' books all the time. Deepak's latest book is plastered with testimonials from Wayne, Marianne, and Jack. Wayne's latest book is plastered with testimonials from Deepak, Marianne, and Jack. Marianne's latest book is plastered with testimonials from Deepak, Wayne, and Jack.

They do it because it works. So we should take the tip and do it, too.

And don't just stop with other people in the psychic/metaphysical community. You can get TONS of great referrals from other people as well. Feel free to think outside the box on this.

For example, how about hairdressers and manicurists? They're sitting around talking to other women all day. They should be talking about you!

Go down to the salon at a slow time of day and offer free readings to the staff if they'll let you leave some business cards or flyers. What do you think they'll all be talking about for the rest of the day, or maybe for the rest of the week?

Let's brainstorm a bit on this. Right now, list ten types of people that might be a great source of referrals for you. I put in hairdressers and manicurists already to get you started, but add in as many as you can think of.

1. Hairdressers
2. Manicurists
3. _____
4. _____
5. _____
6. _____
7. _____
8. _____
9. _____
10. _____

The perfect end result should be that, no matter where your potential client may be looking, no matter what trusted resource she may turn to, she finds that you are the recommended psychic. So who is she going to go to?

One final note: the great majority of the people who read this book will consider this bit of advice and think, "Yes, what a great idea. I really should do it. Maybe I'll start on it tomorrow."

And five years later they find themselves in the 99% who are struggling and they'll be thinking, "Gee, I bought that book; why aren't I making a ton of money?"

Why don't you decide right now to be the person who ends up in that top 1%, and figure out and start implementing those formal referral systems right now? Remember, referrals are the fastest, cheapest, and best ways to get new clients. If you got on this today you could be getting calls for readings tomorrow. It's up to you!

Books and Articles

Writing books and articles is almost as crucial to success in the professional psychic field as creating referral systems. Every single psychic who is earning six figures or more per year has gotten published one way or another. It's not WHAT they published as much as it is simply that they GOT published.

Why? Because getting published gives you national visibility and recognition. In turn, this is what will make you attractive as a potential guest to TV talk shows, and so forth.

Getting published also raises your credibility and can help establish you as an expert in your field.

Start by reading what others have written. Get a feel for the types of books and articles that are popular and successful.

Then write short articles for metaphysical websites. Tell stories about your own metaphysical experiences, readings that you've done (leave out anything that might identify your clients, of course), or techniques for people to develop their own abilities.

If the editors will allow it, put your website address as part of your byline. This way your could attract people to your website, where they would find information as to how to contact you for readings.

Write more general articles for mainstream magazines and newspapers. Try general articles about ghosts and haunted houses in October or articles about angels near to Christmas. Do a survey of people's beliefs in psychic abilities or the paranormal for a general interest story. Write an article about celebrities' beliefs in or use of astrology or other "new age" topic.

You could also start a blog, as discussed above. Log in to your blog every now and then tell stories or write little "how-to" articles. This will give you more practice in writing, and help you build up a collection of writings that you might be able to later put together into a book.

If you don't feel confident or interested in writing, there are still ways to get your words published in these days of high technology.

There are computer programs (often included in the operating system, like the Windows "Sound Recorder" program) that can transcribe your spoken words. You plug in a microphone, and the program will type your words as fast as you speak them with up to 99% accuracy.

If you don't feel computer-savvy enough to do that, there are transcription services that can do it for you for a fee on a per minute or word basis. Just speak into a digital recorder, send them the digital file (and the fee), and they'll type it up for you.

Tape and transcribe your readings, workshops and seminars, too! Many teachers put out books these days that are really not much more than transcribed speaking events.

Articles or Books About or Referencing You

Another way to get into print is to get other people to write about you, or at least to quote you in their own articles and books.

Let your local papers and on-line publications know about your areas of expertise. Send them a professional press release every time you open a new business, schedule a seminar, complete a survey or study of psychic abilities, go on a ghost hunt, hold a séance, publish a book, or whatever.

Most publications are ravenous for new content, and you're in a fascinating and relatively poorly-covered field. Take advantage of this and make yourself easily available. Give interviews, and establish yourself as the local authority on all things psychic. And always mention your website, where people can go to get "more information" about the topic.

Website(s)

A website is truly a necessity these days. Even if it's just a small, one-page site that you set up on MySpace or FaceBook, you need to have someplace on the Internet where people can go to get more information about you, and particularly to find your contact information so they can call you and set up a reading.

Beyond containing basic contact info, though, the potentials for websites are huge, and at some point you'll want to take advantage of those potentials. Things that can be on a website include:

- Listings and descriptions of your services and credentials

- Photos of you, your workspaces, and your tools

- Articles by you about psychic or metaphysical topics

- Videos of you, perhaps showing you doing readings, or talking directly to the camera about yourself and your services

- Items for sale, such as DVDs, CDs, books, metaphysical items like crystal balls, readings done through the Internet, and so forth – basically anything you can sell in-person you can sell on-line, and the process can be automated so that your website is doing sales while you're sleeping or relaxing at the beach

- A sign-up box for your monthly newsletter, which can be sent out to thousands of people by email with just a click of a button

The best thing about websites is that they are dirt-cheap and they can have loads of information on them. Moreover, people now expect you to have one, so they can go get more info about you. Traditional magazine and other printed ads are costly and don't have room for much info. If you have a website you can buy small ads in print media and then just refer people to the sites.

Free Talks and Demos

Short free talks are a great way to raise your visibility and attract possible clients, and they can be done almost anywhere and be about almost anything.

A good speaking opportunity is sometimes found at psychic fairs and expos. Organizers will often set aside a space for such presentations, which can go on during the day. Sometime these speaking opportunities are freely available to people participating in the event, while some events will charge a fee to speakers.

I remember, I once went to a Whole Life Expo held in Santa Monica and celebrity psychic Kenny Kingston had a booth, and he also made a 20 minute presentation on auras in one of the speaker areas. At the conclusion of his presentation he invited people to come to his booth where they could get readings from him at a "show special" price, which in Kenny's case was $50 for 15 minutes. There was a line at his booth for the rest of the day.

Always feel free to think outside the box as far as speaking opportunities go. Remember, almost half the population already believes in psychic abilities, according to recent surveys, and all those people aren't hanging out at the local metaphysical center. You need to go other places to find them.

For example, mainstream bookstores can be another place for short talks. If you're pretty familiar with a number of books on metaphysical topics, make an offer to a bookstore manager that you'll do a little presentation at his store about the metaphysical books he's selling. In exchange, of course, you'll get to tell the people a little bit about yourself and hand out some business cards.

Or how about giving a presentation to a chamber of commerce meeting about how to use intuition (a better word than "psychic abilities" for regular business folk) to increase sales or improve their stock picks?

Or a talk for a singles group about how to find your soul mate? Or a presentation to college age people about discovering their life path?

As I hope is becoming clear, there are many, many opportunities for these kinds of short talks, all of which give you an opportunity to meet lots of potential clients and hand out those business cards.

Paid Lectures, Seminars and Classes

Paid lectures and classes can have the same benefit as short talks, but your credibility is enhanced because either the attendees or the organization putting on the presentation is actually paying you to speak.

Good opportunities for this can be found at metaphysical bookstores and churches, but with a little work you can find some mainstream opportunities as well, such as in college, adult education, and community groups.

There are many groups in your community that are always looking for new and entertaining speakers. You can locate these groups by looking at your local newspapers or websites covering local events. Notice the groups that seem to offer a constant flow of speakers on a variety of topics. Guess what? They need more speakers for next month, next year, and so on. You could become one of their favorites! Contact the group and find out who arranges the speakers, and see if there's a topic you can talk on that would be appropriate for their group.

Start Your Own Group

Having trouble finding a group to speak for? No problem – start your own!

Advertise in local media or at community centers for people interested in attending presentations on metaphysical topics.

When you have enough people indicating interest, then go ahead and start scheduling meetings.

There's a website on the Internet that is specifically designed to help people start groups like this called Meetup.com. Over the years I've organized several Meetup groups that hosted meetings on a variety of metaphysical topics. When I served as a minister I also started a Meetup group for church activities and services, which brought in lots of new people.

Home Parties

As discussed above, home psychic parties are a great way to make extra cash, but they can also be a great way of marketing yourself as well.

For example, at the party, you may have the hostess and ten guests. Each of those guests is going to get a short 10-15 minute reading as part of the party. But each of those guests also could be someone who may want a longer private reading at another time, may want to host a party of her own, may be able to give you referrals, and so forth. So be sure to bring plenty of business cards to hand out to them so they can contact you to arrange those.

Mainstream Events

Psychics may be able to work, or at least create a marketing presence, at many mainstream events such as swap meets and street fairs. The fact that one rarely sees psychics at these types of events doesn't necessarily mean that they are prohibited, but likely rather reflects that most psychics don't understand the marketing potential of those events.

Even if the event producers won't allow readings for money to be done at the event, quite often you may be allowed to set up an "informational" booth that can provide an opportunity to distribute business cards and flyers.

For example, consider a booth at a swap meet with signs saying, "Are You Psychic? Take The Survey!" When people approach the booth they are presented with a questionnaire that lists a bunch of psychic awareness experiences ("Have you ever known who was calling when your phone rang?") and surveys whether they have ever had any those experiences. And, of course, they are given business cards and flyers advertising the next psychic development class you're presenting.

Should anyone ask whether you're a professional psychic, you reply "yes" (of course) and give them one of your business cards and encourage them to call you to set up a reading.

For the above example, by the way, you might also want to consider collating the results of the surveys you get and write an article around it and see if any of the local papers are interested in publishing it. They may not pay much but the publicity could be priceless.

Newsletters

Newsletters can be a great way to market yourself. They can be done on-line on the Internet, by paper-printing and hand distribution, or both. Start out small, and include a couple of stories and articles, and of course be sure to promote yourself and your services. As your subscription list grows, you may be able to sell advertising to others that will help pay for the newsletter.

For the paper-printed version, get permission from local bookstores, metaphysical centers, markets, and other community centers to leave stacks of the newsletter out for their customers to take. If you find a good location that seems reluctant to allow you to leave your literature, offer them free advertising in the newsletter for compensation.

Youtube Videos

One of the most popular websites on the Internet is called Youtube (www.youtube.com) where people can upload videos for free that they have made for other people to watch. And watch they do – by the millions.

You could make a video of yourself, perhaps speaking before a group, giving a reading, teaching a class, demonstrating a technique, or whatever, and include your contact info at the end, and then upload it to Youtube. And if it was a fun video that became popular, it could draw quite a crowd, and all those people would learn about you and what you do and how to contact you. And all at no real cost to you!

CDs and DVDs

Another inexpensive way to market yourself is to make instructional or meditation CDs or DVDs that you give away or sell very cheaply that also promote your readings and classes.

If you have a CD or DVD "burner" it is relatively cheap and easy to make CDs and DVDs, requiring mostly personal time and effort rather than a large cash outlay. Even with a nice color-printed cover you probably won't spend more than a dollar or two apiece to create them.

Personal Billboards

"Personal billboards" refers to clothing, car signs, personalized license plates, tote bags, etc., that have your advertising info printed on them. These can be very effective at attracting a lot of attention at comparatively little cost.

How about:

- A t-shirt that says "Psychics Do It With Spirit"?

- A tote bag that advertises your readings?

- A license plate frame or magnetic car sign advertising your website name and address?

- A baseball cap that says "Tarot Instructor"?

Any of these can be obtained pretty cheaply and easily, but while displayed they will generate continuing interest and inquiries with no other effort on your part. Just keep your business cards handy and be ready to respond to spontaneous inquiries.

Traditional Advertising

Traditional advertising for professional psychics could include placing ads in new age magazines, television and radio ads, ads in the Yellow Pages and other phonebooks, direct mail campaigns, and so forth.

Most of these methods are relatively expensive, and – with respect to marketing professional readings - generally don't have the same pull as many of the methods we've discussed above.

Furthermore, these types of advertising were generally created to market to the masses, which isn't really appropriate for individual reading clients. Professional psychics using Yellow Page ads will usually get some response, but not too much should be expected.

On the other hand, if you're a public speaker or performer whose name is capable of drawing large crowds, then traditional marketing methods would more likely be the way to go as far as promoting your next presentation at the convention center. And we hope that someday that may be a reality for you, if that's your path to success.

Conclusion and Further Recommended Reading

Thank you <u>very much</u> for reading this book. This is a field that I care about passionately, and I am always genuinely thrilled and excited for each new person who finds their way to this path.

I maintain a website for a variety of metaphysical topics, including psychic development, at www.Mystic-Soul.com, and I'd love to have you drop by and check it out sometime. There is also a link from that website to my blog, where I post my related thoughts, experiences, videos and so forth. I also have a website for my readings at www.ReadingsByRob.com, and a website for my past live regression sessions at www.PastLifeSecrets.com.

If you have follow-up questions from the topics discussed in this book, or about other experiences that you have had, please feel free to contact me and I'll be happy to discuss them with you.

The topics of psychic development, psychic reading methods, and marketing professional psychic reading services have been well explored by many other admirable writers.

I have read all of these books and found them useful, and I present them here for your consideration. I hope some of them may serve you as well.

Abadie, M.J. (1995) *Your Psychic Potential* Holbrook, MA: Adams Media Corporation

Bendit, Phoebe Daphne and Bendit, Laurence John (1958) *Our Psychic Sense : A Clairvoyant and a Psychiatrist Explain How It Develops* Wheaton, IL: The Theosophical Publishing House

Bernd, Jr., Ed (2000) *José Silva's Ultramind ESP System* Franklin Lakes, NJ: The Career Press

Bodine, Echo L. (2001) *A Still, Small Voice: A Psychic's Guide to Awakening Intuition* Novato, CA: New World Library

Bristol, Claude M. (1948) *The Magic of Believing* New York, NY: Simon & Schuster

Brown, Courtney, Ph. D. (2005) *Remote Viewing : The Science and Theory of Nonphysical Perception* Farsight Press

Bullis, Ronald (2001) *Sacred Calling, Secular Accountability: Law and Ethics in Complementary and Spiritual Counseling* New York, NY: Routledge

Davidow, Jenny (1996) *Embracing Your Subconscious* Aptos, CA: Tidal Wave Press

Day, Laura (1996) *Practical Intuition: How to Harness the Power of Your Instinct and Make It Work for You* New York, NY: Broadway Books

Day, Laura (1997) *Practical Intuition for Success: A Step-By-Step Program to Increase Your Wealth Today* New York, NY: HarperCollins

Day, Laura (2000) *Practical Intuition in Love : Let Your Intuition Guide You to the Love of Your Life* New York, NY: Perennial Press

Einstein, Patricia (1997) *Intuition - The Path to Inner Wisdom* Boston, MA: Element Books, Inc.

Emery, Marcia (1994) *Dr. Marcia Emery's Intuition Workbook: An Expert's Guide to Unlocking the Wisdom of Your Subconscious Mind* Paramus, NJ: Prentice Hall

Emery, Marcia (2001) *PowerHunch!: Living an Intuitive Life* Hillsboro, OR: Beyond Words Publishing

Feather, Sally Rhine and Schmicker, Michael (2005) *The Gift: ESP, the Extraordinary Experiences of Ordinary People* New York, NY: St. Martin's Press

Ferguson, Gail (2000) *Cracking the Intuition Code: Understanding and Mastering Your Intuitive Power* New York, NY: McGraw-Hill/Contemporary Books

Franquemont, Sharon (2000) *You Already Know What to Do: Ten Invitations to the Intuitive Life* New York, NY: Jeremy P. Tarcher/Putnam

Friedlander, John and Hemsher, Gloria (1999) *Basic Psychic Development : A User's Guide to Auras, Chakras, and Clairvoyance* Boston, MA: Weiser Books

Gawain, Shakti (2001) *Developing Intuition: Practical Guidance for Daily Life* Novato, CA: New World Library

Gee, Judee (1999) *Intuition: Awakening Your Inner Guide* Boston, MA: Weiser Books

Goldberg, Philip (1985) *The Intuitive Edge: Understanding and Developing Intuition* New York, NY: Jeremy P. Tarcher/Putnam

Guiley, Rosemary Ellen (2001) *Breakthrough Intuition: How to Achieve Life of Abundance by Listening to the Voice Within* New York, NY: Berkley Pub Group

Hewitt, William W. (1996) *Psychic Development for Beginners* St. Paul, MN: Llewellyn Publications

Hite, Sheilaa (2003) *Secrets of a Psychic Counselor* Needham, MA: Moment Point Press, Inc.

Hoffman, Enid (1981) *Develop Your Psychic Skills* Atglen, PA: Whitford Press

Holzer, Hans (1997) *Are You Psychic? Unlocking the Power Within* Garden City Park, NY: Avery Publishing Group, Inc.
Ickes, Ph.D., William (2003) *Everyday Mind Reading* New York, NY: Prometheus Books

Jackson, Gerald (1989) *Executive ESP* New York, NY: Simon & Schuster

Jette, Christine (2003) *Professional Tarot: The Business of Reading, Consulting and Teaching* Woodbury, MN: Llewellyn

Johnson, Steven (2004) *Mind Wide Open : Your Brain and the Neuroscience of Everyday Life* New York, NY: Simon & Schuster

Jordan, Ralph D. (1999) *Psychic Counselor's Guidebook : Ethics, Tools, and Techniques* Kailua-Kona, HI: Inner Perceptions, Inc.

Karges, Craig (1999) *Ignite Your Intuition: Improve Your Memory, Make Better Decisions, Be More Creative and Achieve Your Full Potential* Deerfield Beach, FL: Health Communications, Inc.

Keen, Linda (1998) *Intuition Magic: Understanding Your Psychic Nature* Charlottesville, VA: Hampton Roads Pub. Co.

Klein, Gary (2002) *Intuition at Work: Why Developing Your Gut Instincts Will Make You Better at What You Do* New York, NY: Doubleday

Manning, D.D., Al G. (1966) *Helping Yourself with E.S.P.* West Nyack, NY: Parker Publishing Company

Morwyn (2000) *The Complete Book of Psychic Arts* St. Paul, MN: Llewellyn Publications

Nicols, Joe (1998) *How To Make A Good Living As A Professional Psychic* Tranquility Press

Orloff, Judith (1997) *Second Sight* New York, NY: Warner Books, Inc.

Orloff, Judith (2001) *Dr. Judith Orloff's Guide to Intuitive Healing: Five Steps to Physical, Emotional, and Sexual Wellness* New York, NY: Three Rivers Press

Page, Christine (1998) *Beyond the Obvious: Bringing Intuition Into Our Awakening Consciousness* Saffron Walden, UK: The C.W. Daniel Company Ltd.

Palmer, Helen (editor) (1998) *Inner Knowing : Consciousness, Creativity, Insight, and Intuition* New York, NY: Jeremy P. Tarcher/Putnam

Peirce, Penney (1997) *The Intuitive Way : A Guide to Living from Inner Wisdom* Hillsboro, OR: Beyond Words Publishing, Inc.

Prophet, Elizabeth Clare (1997) *Access the Power of Your Higher Self* Corwin Springs, MT: Summit University Press

Radin, Ph.D., Dean (1997) *The Conscious Universe : The Scientific Truth of Psychic Phenomenon* New York, NY: HarperCollins

Radin, Ph.D., Dean (2006) *Entangled Minds : Extrasensory Experiences in a Quantum Reality* New York, NY: Paraview Pocket Books

Reed, Ph.D., Henry (1988) *Awakening Your Psychic Powers* New York, NY: St. Martin's Press

Reed, Ph.D., Henry (1989) *Edgar Cayce on Channeling Your Higher Self* New York, NY: Warner Books

Rhine, J.B. and Brier, Robert (editors) (1968) *Parapsychology Today* New York, NY: Citadel Press

Rhine, J.B. et al. (1940) *Extra-Sensory Perception After Sixty Years* New York, NY: Henry Holt and Company

Rhine, Louisa E. (1967) *ESP in Life and Lab : Tracing Hidden Channels* Toronto, Ontario: MacMillan Company

Ridgeway, Andrei (1999) *Psychic Living : Tap Into Your Psychic Potential* New York, NY: Kensington Books

Roberts, Jane (1966) *How to Develop Your ESP Power* New York, NY: Simon & Schuster

Robinson, Lynn A. (2001) *Divine Intuition* New York, NY: DK Publishing

Robinson, Lynn (2003) *Compass Of The Soul: 52 Ways Intuition Can Guide You To The Life Of Your Dreams* Kansas City, MO: Andrews McMeel Publishing

Rosanoff, Nancy (1988) *Intuition Workout* Boulder Creek, CA: Aslan Publishing

Schnabel, Jim (1997) *Remote Viewers: The Secret History of America's Psychic Spies* Dell Publishing

Schulz, Mona Lisa (1999) *Awakening Intuition: Using Your Mind-Body Network for Insight and Healing* New York, NY: Three Rivers Press

Silva, José and Miele, Philip (1977) *The Silva Mind Control Method* New York, NY: Simon & Schuster

Silva, José and Stone, Robert B. (1989) *You the Healer* Tiburon, CA: HJ Kramer Inc

Silva, José and Stone, Ph.D., Robert B. (1989) *The Silva Mind Control Method for Getting Help from Your Other Side* New York, NY: Simon & Schuster

Stearn, Jess (1976) *The Power of Alpha-Thinking -- Miracle of the Mind* New York, NY: William Morrow and Company, Inc.

Stone, Robert B. (1998) *Life Without Limits* St. Paul, MN: Llewellyn Publications

Vaughan, Frances (1979) *Awakening Intuition* New York, NY: Anchor Books

Walters, J. Donald (2002) *Intuition for Starters* Nevada City, CA: Crystal Clarity Publishers

Wolman, Benjamin B. (editor) (1977) *Handbook of Parapsychology* New York, NY: Van Nostrand Reinhold

Woodruff, Frederick (1998) *Secrets of a Telephone Psychic* Hillsboro, OR: Beyond Words Publishing

CPSIA information can be obtained at www.ICGtesting.com
Printed in the USA
LVOW12s1522230214

374836LV00020B/684/P